T0095427

Fort Chastity, Vietnam, 1969

A Nurse's Story of the Vietnam War

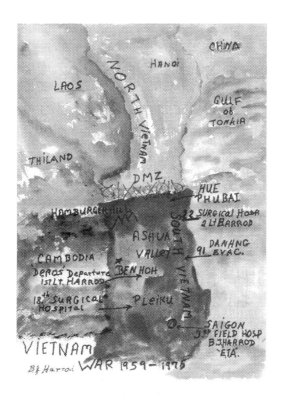

Bernadette J. Harrod, RN

FORT CHASTITY, VIETNAM, 1969
A NURSE'S STORY OF THE VIETNAM WAR

iUniverse books may be ordered through booksellers or by contacting:

iUniverse
1663 Liberty Drive
Bloomington, IN 47403
www.iuniverse.com
1-800-Authors (1-800-288-4677)

Because of the dynamic nature of the Internet, any web addresses or links contained in this book may have changed since publication and may no longer be valid. The views expressed in this work are solely those of the author and do not necessarily reflect the views of the publisher, and the publisher hereby disclaims any responsibility for them.

Any people depicted in stock imagery provided by Thinkstock are models, and such images are being used for illustrative purposes only. Certain stock imagery © Thinkstock.

ISBN: 978-1-4917-7393-2 (sc)
ISBN: 978-1-4917-7395-6 (hc)
ISBN: 978-1-4917-7394-9 (e)

Print information available on the last page.

iUniverse rev. date: 07/31/2015

This book is for all the nurses who served in Vietnam. Thank you. Welcome home. It is dedicated especially to eight nurses who didn't come home. May God please be with us all.

Contents

A Note to the Reader

I am a nurse, not a seasoned author. This is my first book. Please be patient with my short, caustic style and search for the deeper meaning behind the poignancy and the staccato.

Because the army and Vietnam experiences are associated with so much jargon, I suggest that readers first review the glossary.

I have enclosed a military map of Vietnam. The dotted lines denote the division of the I Corps operations within the war-torn country of Vietnam.

My letters home and my poems are my gifts to you.

Introduction

The gravest sin of the women who served in Vietnam is that we haven't told our stories; we have let others tell them for us. Ten thousand nurses and ten thousand stories came out of Nam, and I must share my tale. I have a great need to cleanse myself, to purge my soul of that experience so I can move on.

I will take the risk and stand up and tell my story. Maybe then you will appreciate the horror, envision the twisted bodies, and understand the lives we sacrificed for the war against Communism in a strange dark jungle thousands of miles away from home. Meanwhile, crowds of long-haired hippies mocked our involvement, sneered at our patriotism, and asked, "Why did you go anyway?"

I need to speak out now to free the twenty-four-year-old nurse deep in my being. She has a voice that can no longer be silenced.

The greatest tragedy for the nurses who served in Vietnam is that our story has gone untold, unrecognized, and, for the most part, unknown. My duty as a survivor of the Vietnam War is to inform others about my pain, longing, and sadness, to tell the story of one who has been "in country" and has come home

Bernadette Harrod, RN, ANC

Opening

Many were wounded in Vietnam, and I was one of them. The silence has been the second wound, a festering old wound that cries out for cleaning and air.

I break my silence to stand up and be counted, for and part of my healing is to acknowledge what it was like to be in Vietnam as a nurse, a woman, and a survivor.

These words are written so that you may know my story and so that I may know my pain and begin my healing.

I hope you enjoy my journey and that you will never have to go where I have been and that peace will be with us all.

Why Did I Go?

"Why did you go?" is the question I often hear. I do not know why you cannot understand. I grew up with John F. Kennedy, and his words were burned into my soul. When Vietnam was on fire, I chose the side of the patriots who responded when Uncle Sam called them to go.

When I was little, I went to bed every night with my six-gun slung on my bedpost. So it was only natural that this young Annie Oakley heard the distant call and battle cry of the wounded warriors in Southeast Asia.

It was 1969, and at the time I was a full-fledged operating room (OR) nurse. I had graduated from a three-year diploma program in nursing in 1966 and had stayed at that hospital, the Faulkner, to train as an OR nurse. To the army, I had a critical MOS (military occupational specialty). OR nurses and nurse anesthetists were premium catches for the front. You can't do an operation without an RN to keep track of sponges and equipment and assist the anesthetist. Thus the great number of nurses in Vietnam were like me—OR and critical-care nurses.

I called the army to voice my interest. And I was courted, signed, sealed, and delivered to Vietnam six weeks after signing on the dotted line.

The Setting

The valley was beautiful. The mountains loomed in the distance. The Twenty-Second Surgical Hospital (Twenty-Second Surg.) was nestled in the country among the villages. Rainbows were prevalent; we enjoyed one almost every night. Going out to see the rainbows was a gift. People had peace symbols on their helmets, and one night in the dark, Mary (a hippie-type nurse) painted the new wooden mess hall with love flowers. Everywhere there were posters that read, "War is harmful for flowers and other living things."

Yet there we were, young patriots answering the call to fight the spread of Communism. The inconsistency, the lack of validation was with us even in Vietnam, which we referred to as "in country." We weren't sure about our purpose or our mission. The seed of doubt was within us, and when we returned to a nation hostile toward the war—forgotten and denied any glory for our efforts and the enormous loss of limbs and life—we were angry.

The entire country suffered from posttraumatic stress syndrome (PTSD). The United States was in denial about the war, and as a country responded with a horrendous drug and alcohol problem and a loss of spiritual values. I find it very sad, and I mourn a country that denies its soldiers, its aging parents, and thinks only of me, me, me.

Initial Shockwave ok with move

It was a war fought by babies. The average age of the men was nineteen. They were mostly black and Hispanic city kids and poor midwestern farm boys. I didn't operate on any lawyers or accountants or medical residents. This was a war of teenagers—poor lower-class men who gave their lives and their limbs. I'll never forget their eyes.

I wasn't prepared to work on POWs or to take incoming rounds. There had been no warning that I would operate on Charlie (nickname for a North Vietnamese soldier) or that the Red Cross on our hospital would not be respected by the Vietcong (VC). Six weeks of basic training at Fort Sam Houston, Texas, was not enough preparation for the enormity of the injuries, hours of work, and scope of responsibilities. There was no reprieve or escape. There were three OR nurses, and we worked twelve-hour days, six days a week—more when there was a push.

Hamburger Hill was an unrelenting bloodbath that resulted in numerous double and triple amputees. The moral dilemma of treating the soldiers or letting them slip away was one we faced every day. When a body is blown apart and you have to piece it back together, you ask yourself, "For what? So they can commit suicide later on? So their families can turn away in horror?" After a while, the ceaseless parade of trauma victims made me shut down and just operate. After a few months, I didn't look over the OR drapes to see the faces of the wounded soldiers. I concentrated on the operation at hand and depersonalized the surgery.

Even so, the anger at the devastation rose to fury, but as a nurse, I couldn't grab an M-16 and go out and kill a few "gooks." There was no respite for the horror that surrounded me every day. Today, I am surprised at the number of people who thought nurses carried guns. Maybe if we had struck back instead of shut down emotionally, we would have been better off.

Shakespeare says "to suffer the slings and arrows of outrageous fortune or to take up arms against a sea of troubles." I remember wanting to take an M-16 and open fire, to take revenge, to retaliate. I dealt with the effects of combat but was never able to strike back. It would have helped if I'd carried a gun, but that was not my role. I am a woman, a nurse, a caregiver, a lifesaver.

I stood covered with mud and blood, sweat and tears, serving my country in a war-torn jungle far away from home.

Vietnam Experience

Nam was a collection of people serving their own time, fighting their own war. Even in the hospital unit, we were all strangers to each other. We all came and went out of Nam at different times. Some were "short"; some were "cherry" (new). There was very little esprit de corps. The short-timers hung together, and the new in country fostered friendships among themselves.

The nurses had little to do with the donut dollies. We felt we worked harder than they did, and we were too tired at the end of the day to chitchat with them anyway. The enlisted men (EMs) stuck together, and the docs were the docs. They had been drafted and were unhappy to be there. The nurses were older than most of the EMs, better educated, and officers. The ratio of EMs to nurses was so high, the system forced the nurses to retreat to our hooches to avoid the huge numbers of men. Nam was different. Everyone was fighting his or her own personal war and focused on his or her own DEROS, which stood for "date eligible for return from overseas." There was no group consciousness.

Without a front line to fight on, the war took place in a series of base camps. Platoons fought for areas, gave them up, and tried to regain them for control at a later date, if necessary.

Enemy soldiers would be brought to our hospital half blown away. We would operate, and they would go to the holding ward guarded by the Army of the Republic of Vietnam (ARVN), the South Vietnamese Army. When we were hit, it was because we had a high-ranking Vietcong officer in our holding ward. I was neither prepared for nor able to cope with this manner of war. We were surrounded by chaos. The country was out of control. Enemy soldiers looked the same as ARVN troops. Women and babies— innocent victims—were caught in the crossfire in neighboring villages.

The worst memory I have of Phu Bai,where the hospital was located, is of the day we did a C-section on a mother who had been hit in a nearby village. We delivered the baby dead. He caught a frag between the eyes and was killed in utero. The memory burns, an indelible mark that may never be erased.

In-Country Experience

Phu Bai was all right—that is, if you liked mud in the rainy season and dust during the dry season.

Life for the nurses at Phu Bai was at best primitive. Our hooches were small, wooden structures divided into four rooms. You could hear every conversation in the adjoining room. We each had a screen door and one window and a cot to sleep in. We had no fans or air conditioners. We did have the only flush toilet on base—the "it" toilet. The showers were wooden, bug-invested spider havens. The bugs in Nam were big IAGREE TO WRITE OUT SOS. ALSO SAY IT WAS CREAMED HAMBURGER ON A WHITE SAUCE PUT ON A PIECE OF TOASTenough to throw a saddle on. The mess hall was a tent that served dried eggs and a variety of unpalatable slop. We dunked our tray in a rinse bath and soapy water on our way out of the mess hall.

Nam was dry and hot, 120–130°F half of the year. The sweat would just pour off me. The second half of the year, December to March, was wet due to the monsoons. It would rain for days, weeks, and months. I was always wet—with sweat, rain, or blood. For fourteen months I showered with bugs, slept on a cot, and dined on dried food.

Letters from home and care packages kept me going. Mom sent me brownies, a box of "Fishes," and a tape recording from all my brothers and sisters. I had a small reel-to-reel recorder, and I would listen to their voices and cry. Making a tape to send home was difficult. There was no good news to tell, and the sound of distant bombing would have scared my mother.

The Twenty-Second Surg. was on a plot of land no bigger than a football field. There was no place to go. You couldn't take a walk to the perimeter and back. The lack of space, both personal and community, was very restrictive. The living situation was ancestral. We ate, slept, worked, and partied together. There was no retreat. The only escape was internal: you had to block down and become a hermit in your hooch.

My Phu Bai experience encompassed a number of significant traumatic events. We were under threat of attack because the hospital

7

was the furthest north on the evacuation chain. Hospitals were not considered sacrosanct by the enemy. We were a Surgical MUST (Medical Unit, Self-Contained and Transportable). We sat on the cusp of the Huế border, ten miles south of the DMZ. Our hospital consisted of five inflated Quonset hut–type wards and four boxlike operating rooms. We had a holding ward for wounded Vietnamese. The ARVN and US intelligence officials would interrogate them before sending them to the ARVN hospital to ensure that they were not VC. The hospital received four mortar attacks during my fourteen-month stay. I was horrified that we would be shelled because I thought we were protected by the Geneva Convention.

The Twenty-Second Surg.'s function was to save life and limb. We opened bellies, did temporary colostomies, and removed arms and legs. Every operation was so bloody, we had to work hours to hose down after surgery. Our patients only stayed two to three days, until they were medically stable enough to move to an evacuation hospital. As an OR nurse, I never saw the fruits or the consequences of our labors. The patients were medevaced out of the surgical hospital to the evacuation hospital in Chu Lai and then to Japan or Hawaii and eventually home. There was no closure to what I did in Nam, and there never has been. It seeps and pulsates like an open wound. And I wonder if I will ever meet the boys on whom we operated. Will I ever close the circle?

We never talked about our feelings or what happened that day in the OR. We went from a bloodbath to a beer bash. War was hell, and we were the "round eyes" invited to every function in I Corps. The marines, the Seabees, and the officers at the Twenty-Second Surg. were always having barbecues, and we were expected to go to those functions. Fuel barrels were split lengthwise and used as hibachis to grill the chicken. Beer and booze flowed like water, and the round eyes were sought after by every American GI, officer or EM, married or not. If you weren't an alcoholic already, being in country helped you on your way. It was a sure quick fix for forgetting the pain. We partied like there wouldn't be any tomorrow.

I was in a purely chaotic situation. Never before had I been sought after (I invited someone to my junior prom). Now, I was a movie star! I couldn't cope, and I was tired and ill prepared for the horror all around me. I needed someone to depend on and protect me. I found the chaplain's assistant a real doll. He had the midwestern twang and broad shoulders, and was a college graduate. So I did the obvious thing. I married him! In a war-torn country, I married an enlisted man. It helped me survive the chaos. Once I was Leo's wife, I had the love and respect and friendship of the EMs on the base. I was safe, protected, and totally lost in the love bubble. I could decompress with lovemaking after a hard day in surgery. After all, war was hell.

But there was no reprieve for the nurses. We were stuck working twelve-hour days, six days a week. There was no opportunity to rotate back to a field hospital. I was in country in Phu Bai for fourteen months, living on a plot of a base camp that was no bigger than a football field.

The confinement and the never-ending casualties were so draining that after a while the nurses shut down and remained isolated in their hooches, or they turned into party animals. The Freedom Bird (the plane that returned military personnel to the United States) seems faraway when you're new in country. When I was a newcomer, I involved myself in Med-Cap and visits to the orphanage in Hué. In a way, that was a little escape into normalcy.

One of the nurses had a sewing machine,. and we would sew, and she would sing peace songs on her guitar. No men were allowed. It was girls' night out. Inside the Fort Chastity nurses' barracks, we tried to keep fragments of what and who were intact and alive. Mary played her guitar, Sue sang peace songs, and I learned to play the harmonica … somewhat. And I strung up a clothesline in my hooch and hung up new words and their meanings. I memorized Shakespeare, Thoreau, and Frost when I wasn't saving lives. I formed a running team; we would jog to the perimeter and back each day, round the barrels of burning human feces, build up a sweat, and head back to our own hideaway, Fort Chastity, Phu Bai, Vietnam.

One of the problems of being in Nam is that, mentally, we were never there. We never discussed our day in surgery. We talked about what we did "back in the world" and what we would do when we got out of hell. But we never talked about the present, the now, Nam. Mentally we were home before we left the airport in Da Nang. The denial was like Great Wall of China wall—thick, tall, and never-ending.

To reinforce this, our chief nurse put us on the "invite circuit." We were expected to accompany her up the road to the officers' club at the marine post. As "her girls," we would get all dolled up in our civvies, pack into a jeep, and head up to a strange club, where we were courted by officers we didn't know. They probably had wives and five kids each at home, but for the evening they were all miraculously single. I truly hated those functions—the shame and the deceit. I had dried blood under my fingernails after a busy day in the OR, and yet I was expected to function as a lady and an officer with a bunch of loved-starved strange men.

I don't want to sound like an angry Vietnam vet. It was one of life's intense experiences, and some good comes from every phase, every partaking. What I learned from my Vietnam experience is the value and price of peace. I never take my freedom for granted. Green grass, blue skies, distant clouds, and Big Macs—I cherish them all.

I grew up that year. The experience was invaluable, something to tell my grandchildren. I am different from having served, a little bit more spiritual, a little bit more thankful.

How often did I look over the OR drapes into the trusting eyes of a wounded GI? Those eyes were full of fear. With all the sensitivity in my heart, I would squeeze his young hand under the drapes and say, "You're in good hands now, soldier. You're on the operating table. We'll take good care of you." As he counted backward from ten to one, the sodium pentothal would induce a quiet, sweet sleep. Then we would go to work—cutting off his fatigues, picking off the twigs and dirt from the broken and splintered remains of limbs. Once the flesh was open to the air, I would begin the scrub. The mixture of Phisohex, blood, and bone splinters is with me still—a pink bubbly solution, not unlike brain tissue. The intravenous lines in, the multiple operations would begin—cut, saw, sew, clip, sponge. If the abdomen had a frag wound, we would crack the belly. The blood would gush out, up and over the drapes, soaking us to the skin. Blood products would be pumped under pressure into multiple IV lines. A strategic game of hemo-dynamic equilibrium would begin. We had to replace all the blood we were losing through the wound. "We're losing him," were words heard so often from the nurse anesthetist behind the drapes. "No!" the surgeon would cry. "I almost have homeostasis. More fluids, nurse. Four more units of blood."

We cracked the bellies and removed the arms and legs of oh so many. Young lives. Brave young men, to whom I promised, "You're in good hands, son." And in their sleep, we would dismember their young forms and change their destinies forever.

What we did in surgery was never enough. Some we lost; maybe they were the lucky ones. I often wonder if they remember me and my words of comfort. Did I help, or do they hate me for lying? Because it wasn't okay, and they would never be okay again. They're just so sad— the memories of the Twenty-Second Surg. and the never-ending parade of broken bodies. I am often overcome with guilt because I lied to the soldiers. Were they words of comfort or just words to assuage my own conscience?

I don't know how many amputations we performed in the year I was there. Some guys lost two or even three limbs, both legs and an arm. Those were the saddest cases, those and the mutilating facial injuries. Some of the scenes were so emotionally brutal that my psyche can't call them up. They are lost in a card file without an index to reference. Thank God for that.

I Wonder

I often wonder why I was so shocked at what I saw and heard in Vietnam. After all, I was twenty-four years old when I volunteered. I wasn't a baby! I was a fully trained operating nurse who had seen her share of trauma and death. But there was no preparation for Nam. I went from signing on the dotted line to Phu Bai in seven weeks. My preparation was six weeks of Officer Candidate School at Fort Sam Houston. We learned to march in formation, read a map, even operate on a goat, but that training was not commensurate with the roles and responsibility required at the Twenty-Second Surg.

The day I walked into the OR in Phu Bai I was expected to help with amputations and take care of minor debridement on GIs. I was not prepared to operate on ARVN, VC, or civilians, who all had intestinal worms and hepatitis. Operating on civilians left the OR team at great risk for those diseases and also salmonella. When I had only sixteen weeks to go before DEROS, I became very sick with serum hepatitis B. I spent five weeks in the intensive care unit (ICU)—frail, yellow, lonely, and homesick. I couldn't go to an open ward because I was female, and there were no provisions for females in a war zone. Never have I felt so used or forgotten, left alone, and abandoned to turn yellow and itch. I would beg my doctor to let me go to my hooch, to let me see the sky at least. I was so thin and pale, so spent and fatigued, I could give no more.

Very slowly my liver function improved and the jaundice disappeared. I went back to surgery, but I didn't go at it as hard as I had during the first nine months that I was in country. Like a wounded dog, I shut down, I know I did. The death and destruction of a push didn't put a chink in my armor. I was short now, and I had paid my dues. All I could think about during my last three months in Nam was the big Freedom Bird, home, Mom and Dad, and my brothers and sisters, Wollaston Beach, and a hot bath. I wasn't there emotionally. I was already home. Essentially I was in a gray-out, an emotional shutdown; I became an automatic pilot; I did and acted as I was expected to without any emotional involvement.

I often wonder why I wasn't ready for what went on in Nam. I guess I figured we would only operate on GIs. I wasn't ready when they presented me with ARVNs and POWs to shave and scrub and save. For what? Wasn't Charlie the enemy? After surgery, all the non-Americans would be interrogated in the holding ward to ensure they were really ARVN and not VC before they were transferred to the Provincial Vietnamese Hospital. As a professional nurse, I'd taken an oath to help and heal mankind, but I was reluctant to aid the enemy and totally unprepared for my involvement with CIA interrogations of the enemy. Whenever we had questionable VC high-ranking officers in our holding ward, we could bet there would be "incoming." Charlie would try to wipe out his own before they sang to the intelligence people from the US of A. It was hard to save the lives of those who may have been responsible for previous cases in my OR. I was reluctant to help them, and for that I felt shame and guilt. At times, I wanted to kill the VC. But I couldn't, and for that, I felt hopeless and guilty. Nurses in Nam didn't carry guns.

I guess I was naive but I never thought anyone would shoot me. Wasn't I stationed in a hospital and protected by the Geneva Convention? The day our hospital took our first hit I was in the OR. "Hit the deck! Dive!" someone yelled. "To the floor, Lieutenant." I froze. I was in the middle of an operation. The patient's belly was open, and exposed viscera hung on the drapes. How could I abandon the operative field? By the grace of God, I wasn't killed. The next time I heard the distinctive whistling sound of incoming, I was the first guy on the ground, surgery or no surgery.

Lies My Country Told Me

Before any surgery, I would look over the drapes and ask the soldier, "Where were you hit, son?" "Laos," he might say. I couldn't believe that my country would lie or be deceitful to the general public. The government told us we would not fight in Laos or Cambodia, but I knew different. I was really mad at myself for being so naïve, for volunteering, for being part of the scam. Besides we were losing; I could tell. It was instinctual in a nurse, the way I knew when an operation was going sour, and we were going to lose a patient on the table. I could tell we were losing the war after Hamburger Hill. Nothing could have been more bloody, more costly in life or limb for one small knoll, one small piece of property. In my opinion, we would never pry Charlie from his tunnels of terror. The VC were dug in too far, and we were losing the war.

Trees didn't grow in the woods that surrounded Phu Bai. Occasionally, I'd see fixed-wing air-cargo planes spraying, but I figured they were killing mosquitoes to keep malaria from becoming an epidemic. Several years later, in 1975, I received my first Agent Orange questionnaire in the mail, and I got 100 percent. I couldn't believe that my Uncle Sam would endanger my health and the health of everyone else to defoliate Nam. The long-term effects have not yet been compiled, but we know that depression, infertility, and uterine cancer are some of the health problems caused by Agent Orange. Leave it alone personal accounts.

I can only speak for myself: I tend to get depressed, and it took me six years to conceive my only son. I get angry at my country and the lies I was told. I thought that, as a woman, I would be protected, nurtured, and honored by my country. So far none of those things have happened to female Vietnam veterans. Our lives were at grave risk. Our experience was neither counted nor honored by our government. We had to fight Congress and the Commission of Fine Arts to erect a statue to honor the nurses who served. We were not drug-crazed baby killers or on a man hunt. We were young, wide-eyed patriots who went to help and cure the broken and the wounded.

Common Misconceptions

If you think we were one big happy hospital family, you are wrong. The Twenty-Second Surg. was a MUST building, not a service unit. We didn't all come over at the same time. The Vietnam War was a wholly individual war, and sometime the war was within ourselves.

On one exceptionally hot night, a sergeant was shot by a fellow GI while the two were playing cards. I operated on a GI who had napalm burns on his hand and arm. Someone had slipped him a gift package in the night. The worst operations were on American GIs who had been fragged.

The nurses didn't really speak to or share with each other. We were all so busy or dog-tired after our twelve-hour shifts, we didn't have time or the energy to share our experiences with one another. If there were free time, a nurse spent it with her beau. The nurses in my unit had special boyfriends to protect them from the hungry wolves.

There were Red Cross workers stationed at the hospital, but there was no love lost there. I was risking my life, and they were playing games with the GIs in the dirt. To me, they were inept, starry-eyed social workers who served no real purpose. They were donut dollies. They wore seersucker uniforms and old lady shoes, took rides in helicopters to firebase camps, performed shows, and passed out cookies and bug juice (Kool-Aid) to the GIs. The donut dollies never stayed long. The Red Cross rotated them every three months, but we were stuck in Phu Bai for the duration. As I look back, I realize I was jealous of them—jealous of their freedom, autonomy, and ability to get to know the fighting men on a deeper level than I could. I never took the risk because they would rotate out in three months. I thought, why bother?

So there was no deep, shared experience. For the women who served, Vietnam was a lonely, dirty, little war. Leave alone please.

Coming Home

Ungrateful hearts awaited us. The big Freedom Bird touched down in Seattle, Washington, and a sigh went up from the 168 GIs on board. We cried silent, joyful, grateful tears. I never was so glad to be home, be free to eat a Big Mac or order take-out Chinese, see pine trees, or stroll along an avenue, or to hug my mom and my dad and tell them that I loved them.

The lines to ETS ("estimated time of separation"), i.e., to process out, were long. I was told to change my uniform in the ladies room, and I was bused to the bachelor officers' quarters to wait while the men had a roast beef congratulatory dinner. We never received a "Thank you," a hug, or a "Welcome home, soldier." Instead, I was handed the message "Go over there, and wait some more," and I took it. There was no time to decompress or talk about the horror. I changed from battle fatigues to a dress, and within twenty minutes I'd forgotten Nam. I left it in that ladies room at the airport and went on with my life. But I would never be the same person again. I never talked about the war or its aftermath. After a few people asked me, "Why did you go anyway?" I took the Vietnam experience off my résumé and never mentioned it again.

Thirty years later, the war was remembered, edited, romanticized, and turned into books, movies, and HBO miniseries. What was once a stigma is now a hot item. That's why I came out of the closet—to tell you the true story of what it was like for me, to share a poem and some of my letters home. Once I was lonely, isolated, and forgotten, but now I hope to stop being the silent, invisible force and stand up and be counted as a woman of dignity and honor.

We Are Not Invisible

Nothing divided our country like the Vietnam conflict. Brothers at home marched in protest against brothers fighting in Pleiku, Da Nang, and Phu Bai. Our heroes got spit in their faces as they walked off the Freedom Bird. Green berets were snatched off heads by long-haired pacifists. All the while, our supposedly sacrosanct military hospitals were being rocketed by the VC. The fact that our hospitals were targets for the North Vietnamese Army (NVA) never became part of the antiwar rhetoric.

Who were the drug-craved lunatics? The special forces going behind Loas or the flower children, who went naked into lakes at Woodstock for communal baptisms? Both were surreal!

Back then, we felt the total and complete lack of support back home. Then we received the nonwelcome when we returned. Then we had to wage a slow fight for recognition of the nurses who served. The Veterans Administration and the Vet Centers focused on the men. There were no places for female vets to go. So we did what we learned to do in Nam. We shut down. We ignored our experience and tried to go on with our lives. But denying the pain of this traumatic war experience contributed to a far greater trauma, a second enforced silence. We joined the country in its own PTSD; we created a charade: *Vietnam never happened! Get a big broom, and sweep it under the rug—way under. Let's get on with our life. Go to grad school. Get a hot car. But don't think about your pain.*

Being A Woman In Vietam-1969

The shock of being a woman in a war zone in a foreign country only increased when Vietnamese stared at you because you were tall and round-eyed. The GIs were so hungry; to them I was a woman, a nurse, a sister, a mother, and the girl next door. I developed a personality conflict. *Who the hell was I? Why the hell was I there?* The undercurrent of anger exploded into rage when the hospital took a direct hit from Charlie. My jaded cynicism had a dual cause: being sprayed with unknown herbicides and the rising anti-Vietnamese movement back home.

The peace movement got more press than the war heroes; in country, we fragged our buddies, treated mutilating wounds, and watched the tragedy of innocent mothers and babies die. We watched the loss of innocence with the sense that nothing was sacred or honored. Our hospital was hit; civilians caught in fight between VC and new recruits— we called them DINKs ("desperately in need of knowledge")—with AK 47s. I had nightmares of black pajamas running through the wards carrying satchel charges.

Life was primitive in Nam. The average temperature was 120°F, and it rained buckets for half of the year. Shoes were a joke. I showered with the bugs, slept on a cot, and ate dried eggs. The internal culture shock was always there, but a rash of casualties caused new emotions. Young hopeful men cut down at the beginning of their lives. Devastating casualties! Double and triple amputations!

Maybe we should have let nature take its course. It was only five to eight minutes from the bush to the Twenty-Second Surg. OR suite. We saved many who would have mercifully died in the field. I was changed forever. Nothing can ever compare to the agony, mutilation, courage, and pure grit of those Vietnam War heroes.

Post Traumatic Stress Syndrome

All the nurses who served in Vietnam were victims of war. Our country was too willing to forget. We saw firsthand the horrors and the cost of that conflict, in intensive care units, operating rooms, and open wards. The endless stream of multiple fragment wounds, burns, and amputees haunts us to this day. Whenever I am under stress or undergoing a loss or change, a vivid Vietnam dream reoccurs, reminding me of my powerlessness over uncontrollable situations in my life.

We are more than a fistful of women. Approximately eleven thousand women served during the Vietnam conflict. Yet the Department of Defense neither keeps records of female veterans nor does any official studies on readjustment problems among them. The Veterans Administration offers women little or no medical or psychological assistance. According to the few studies conducted, 20 percent of women who served suffer from flashbacks, depression, alcoholism, and serious emotional, marital, and professional difficulties, according to the book Commemorative of the Vietnamese Womens Memorial.

My heart will always quicken whenever there is a helicopter overhead. No one can see all that I saw—the pain, the massive rejection from my country—and go away unscathed and unscarred.

It was a dirty little war, and no one wanted to be identified with it. When I came home everyone was anti-Vietnam, so I went undercover. I didn't talk about it. Isolation and denial became my coping style too. But I was plagued. I had developed skills in the OR that I could never use stateside. I could clamp and cut and suture. The deep sense of equality that I knew on the OR team was gone forever. I couldn't go through the double doors to surgery anymore and be a second-class citizen, a handmaiden, a passer of instruments. So I did what many others did, despite the skills that they had painfully acquired in Vietnam: I denied my own experience, and I never went into an OR again.

I was a very angry Vietnam vet. I don't deny that. To date, I have not been to the wall, the Vietnam Veterans Memorial in Washington, DC. Who will pick me up when I crumble? Who will support me when the emotions hit me in the face? I will go with a group to see the Vietnam Women's Memorial. I know I can't do it alone—stand by that black wall and remember all the boys who didn't "make it off the table" or left Nam in body bags. Who will be there for me?

Closing the Circle

There is still no closure thirty years later after my tour of duty in 1969. I never saw the results of all our efforts, all the long hours spent over an open belly in the middle of the night. Even though we are medical people, we are strangely affected. We have the same PTSD symptoms of estrangement and isolation. Few of us have come together to share our feelings and break this cycle of terminal uniqueness. We have a real anger at the government because of its lack of preparation, because we were not able to retaliate against the enemy. Few civilians realize that nurses didn't carry guns in Nam. Maybe we would have faired better if we had kicked a little ass. We also suffer from survivor's guilt. What we did will never be enough. If only we had tried harder, worked longer hours. Why did we come home intact when all those men are missing so many arms, so many legs? We never should have gone, or we never should have come home, at least not in one piece.

The overwhelming feelings of hopelessness spill over into my life today. When a push came in Nam, the injured came so fast and so many. They'd arrive in eight to twelve minutes: five litters, ten walking wounded, three expectants, arriving en mass. There were never enough resources or personnel to treat them all at once. We had a deep, sick feeling of powerlessness and hopelessness day after day, no matter how much we gave or what we did. Enough was never enough.

I have a very low tolerance for frustration in my life. I have no patience, not for long lines or commercials on TV. I attack my lawn mower if it fails to turn over after the fourth pull on the starter coil. Idle chatter and empty-headed females LEAVE AS IS THANK YOU make me sick. A voice yells through the lonely corridors of my mind: "Don't mean nothing."

There is a pervasive sadness in my eyes as there is in the eyes of every army or navy nurse, every donut dolly, and every enlisted woman. Those sad eyes reflect the souls of people who have been to hell and back. Our initial idealism ended in disappointment. We went to help, to care for, and to care. But we became entangled in the evil, in the chaos of a dirty war where the enemy was amorphous and the front line was nonexistent. There was no cause and effect in Nam. Years of scientific thinking didn't help in a crisis situation where the volume and sensitivity knob was turned to the hilt. Nam was like a living Dali canvas. What was supposed to be real wasn't. It was a surrealistic walk in the jungle. What was reflected on the retina didn't compute as reality. There was no file for war and its consequences, so what we saw became our reality.

We lost our innocence. Once in country, we were never the same again. The word *war* gained a new and terrible meaning. Even today, I set myself up for hopeless situations against insurmountable odds. I play racket ball with the biggest, toughest guys in the club. Losing is inevitable, and the struggle is always upward. Yet I can't wait to get on the court with them.

I am vigilant and focused. I am also jumpy, oversensitive, and quick to take the blame for any wrong done. As nurses, we need to tap the strengths we developed in Nam. We need to acknowledge our versatility, our grit, and our ability to persevere against all odds. Then we need to reframe our experiences in light of our unique strengths and see the good. After all, we are survivors who also helped others survive.

B.J. Harrod

The war led to different combinations of behavior patterns. For example, I don't like people to be behind me, especially in the dark. I will change my seat two to three times in a movie theater if someone is breathing down my neck. It's a matter or trust. Even at church, I move if things get tight. My sleep has never been the same. I sleep near the door under an open window. I need air at all times. I sleep with one foot outside the covers ready to jump and answer the call: "Lt. Harrod, incoming wounded. You're wanted in surgery." I am very claustrophobic. I don't go into stores where I can't see the exit signs and the lights are too bright. Unexpected sounds make me jump. People who sneak up on me are in for a big surprise. I have frightened a few coworkers with my response.

My jaded "so what, don't mean nothing" attitude surfaces when the bullshit comes down from authority figures. I have never liked bosses, but the sad thing is that everyone has to report to somebody. I have a real problem with authority figures who don't know what's happening on the front line.

I have never met any of the GIs I operated on for hours. I long for the reunion where I'll hold up a sign that says, "22nd Surg—Phu Bai." The GIs I'd worked on would come over, we'd hug and cry, and we'd talk about our lives after Nam. I long to close the circle, and I trust it will happen some day. God willing and in God's time. I must say my prevalent emotion is sadness. We went and gave and no one said, "welcome home" or "thankyou."

PTSD or Not

The damage was subtle. We were made to feel "less than" because our arrival home went unnoticed. This invalidated the pain I suffered as a female survivor. We were forgotten, not even counted as being in Vietnam. There are no complete records of our numbers in Nam as I learned from many educational Vietnam workshops i attended.

PTSD gets worse if victims are not able to speak about their experiences. Until recently, I never spoke about Nam. I pulled myself together and went on with life. The women of Nam only started coming forward in the 1980s. The Vietnam Women's Memorial (dedicated in 1993) is a legacy of healing and hope. For the women who served, the national conferences in 1985 and 1988 sponsored by the Joiner Center of Boston State College, was the very first time they had seen and talked with nurses who had acted in similar capacities. Together we participated to validate our experiences and feelings. We were no longer alone in the realms of our experiences or unique in our responses to those experiences.

I am enjoying the process of being a member of a group of women who served the country during the Vietnam era. Twenty years later the healing has begun for me, and I am right where I am supposed to be. As I am free to speak and write about my feelings, the deeper inner core emerges, and I am free.

Removing the stigma is slow. Nursing is a second-rate profession (forgive me ladies); add the fact that women in the military were labeled as camp chasing, on a manhunt, or lesbians, and the burden is becomes even heavier. Women in the military have been stereotyped. The nurses weren't counted, and our medical records were destroyed; there are no accurate documents of the numbers or types of nursing professionals who gave their lives to serve in Vietnam. Actions speak loudly, and we heard the rejection clearly.

PTSD is short for posttraumatic stress disorder. It is an old phenomenon with a new label. Prolonged, unrelenting chaos and stress can cause delayed reactions in the victims. Nurses were very susceptible to PTSD because we worked very long hours dealing with catastrophic wounds in primitive, life-threatening conditions without any reprieve. We couldn't take up a gun or run away from the horror for a day or a week. Years later PTSD can manifest itself overtly as insomnia, depression, flashbacks, or suicide or more covertly as troubled relationships, divorce, separation, difficulty with intimacy, alcoholism, job hopping.

The PTSD syndrome may affect us all in some areas. I don't blame my life or fate on Nam, and I shy away from catchall diagnoses. But I do feel that every nurse who served must have a hard time ignoring the symptoms.

Post Vietnam

I turned very gray in Nam. My temples were gray beyond my years. Outwardly, I aged so. Now I sometimes *feel* older than my years, like an old, old, person. Nam was the most sobering experience I have ever had. I saw, smelled, and heard such chaos and confusion, such surreal glimpses of the world. There was no place to file them in my memory. Occasionally these visions fall out, and I remember a smell, a sound, an entire scene. It may be just a pair of fearful eyes, that look of promises received, of "Yes, I am all right now." Or it may be the grossest scene— an open belly crawling with intestinal worms, a baby shot dead in utero, a GI sawed in half by a mine explosion. There I'll be, all gowned up, trying to save that poor son-of-a-bitch.

Anything can trigger it. A badly burned patient, a distant Huey (helicopter) breaking through the trees, and I am right back there. The whole thing stays with you for such a long time. I interpret a big cat as a rat. I hate to be closed in, and I can never work with burn victims; the smell triggers too many memories.

Vietnam vets are a close group, because all we have is each other. No one understands to the extent that another Vietnam vet does. Outsiders don't have the frames of reference. But maybe with heightened interest some will come to accept what we saw and did in country.

Something Good Can Come from Any of Life's Experiences

Did anything good come out of my experiences in Vietnam? Something must have. Yes, I survived! If I could survive that horror and go on with my life intact, whole, and functioning, then that proved it. Yes, I am a survivor who helped others survive. Because of the enormous casualties and threats to my life, I have felt invincible, almost indestructible. Nothing phases me. I don't have the average rape fears that many single women have. To me, if there aren't VC in the parking lot running toward me with satchel charges, then I am safe enough.

Once I was home, I disregarded normal precautions. "Don't mean nothing, nothing." Job hassles, personality clashes, and broken relationships seemed like petty disturbances in a world where there were no perimeters and no threats of attack. I could easily throw up a wall to block out pain and become insensitive to horror at a moment's notice. The only problem with walls is, as Frost said, "What are you walling in or walling out?"

Since the Vietnam conflict, I have faced great odds at high stakes, and I didn't mind when I lost. After all, we were losers, weren't we?

Vietnam has made me grateful for my freedom; that is the biggest gift. Every day I know the price of peace. Only one who has seen war can truly know the meaning of peace—a personal peace, knowing that I went, served, saved, and survived—an experience that I can share with those who weren't there or are too young to know. Only the truth will set us free.

Reactions to the Conference: A New Beginning

The conference, Titled Woman of the War, was held from April 29 to May 1, 1988. I didn't want to go. I didn't want to look at or feel the pain. But most of all, I didn't trust that anybody would be there to pick up the pieces. After all, I'd gone to Vietnam alone in February 1968, in the aftermath of the Tet Offensive. I worked long, lonely hours in the mud, amputated countless arms and legs, scooped out eyes, and slashed open bellies in a hurry to stop the bleeding. All that was behind me. I went alone, served alone, and came home alone—alone, isolated, and afraid of what was behind that door that I had bolted shut. On that door read "Vietnam. Don't Enter." Behind it, deep in my psyche, was pain and loss, guilt and remorse, and unrelenting sadness.

So why did I go to the conference? A little tug at my heart kept pulling me toward it. Then an old friend, a former donut dolly, called and said she would be going. That mean I wouldn't have to go alone this time.

The conference was held in the palatial Park Plaza Hotel,Boston, Ma. My knees were shaking; fear was my foremost emotion.

The opening keynote speaker was Mary Stout, then president of the Vietnam Veterans of America. The tall redhead, who had served as a nurse in Vietnam, stood erect; she seemed bigger than life. I will never forget her words: "For all of you who have never been welcomed home, Welcome home. For all of you who have never been thanked, I thank you from the bottom of my heart." I sat in the back row next to a sixty-five-year-old black woman who had served in World War II. I wept old, salty, acid tears from a deep place in my soul. That kind woman reached across my lap and held my hand while I wept. I wasn't alone anymore; I had come home.

This was the end of the isolation for me. The three-day conference enlightened, refreshed, and introduced me to other combat veteran nurses from the Vietnam era. I met nurses like me, who had served and then pulled their lives into perspective and moved on. I met beautiful artists and poets—women of dignity and distinction, published authors and researchers.

By the end of the three days, I had opened up. I shared my vulnerability and my pain. I attended a PTSD workshop knowing that I had touches and traces of the dreaded syndrome, and I met Rose Sandecki, Vietnam veteran team leader, Concord California Vet Center. She spoke about "carrying the torch," making the conference the beginning of the healing process, and being good to ourselves. The group included Dr. Jessica Wolfe from my local Veterans Hospital in Boston. When I raised my hand and shared from my heart, the wellspring came up, and I cried out, "Where do I go from here?" Jessica came up to me after the PTSD breakout session and said three simple words, "I will help." I was filled with gratitude. I had been heard after twenty long years. It meant a new beginning for me, a road back from a deep abyss.

My life has been very different since the conference. I have phone numbers, a support group, and, for once, faces that go with a time I once thought would be best forgotten. Those faces of love and understanding were there with me in the pain and the loss and are with me now in the healing. I can see them and touch them. They have names and dreams and are associated with great accomplishments.

For me, the Second National Conference on Women in the Military was the beginning of the end of isolation.

How Vietnam Changed Me

On the positive side, my wartime experience has made me a hearty camper. I travel lighter. I am not bogged down with material possessions; a simple, uncluttered life suits me fine. I adapt well. If the hot-water heater is broken, I shower in cold water. I love to camp and be outdoors, to run in the rain and dig in the dirt. Bugs don't faze me, and neither do rats. It's embarrassing sometimes. I will squish a spider with my thumb and check to see if someone is looking.

Soon after I returned from Nam, I had to stop myself from emptying an intravenous line or a blood line on the floor. I was used to nursing in a tent, not a plush carpeted ICU.

Nam made me value the simple things, like a tub bath, real eggs, and toast that is hot and freshly buttered. Because of my experiences in a war zone, I know I am a survivor. No matter what life hands me, I always say to myself, "Well, at least there is no incoming."

In Nam, I felt totally appreciated and truly needed. As I have said before, we lived in a very small community no bigger than the size of a football field. We worked together, ate together, watched movies together, and slept together. The absolute feeling of community at the Twenty-Second Surg. was wonderful. Just for fun we'd play volleyball in our underwear. We built a replica of the Golden Gate Bridge over a trickle of a stream in the compound and painted it, naturally, gold. We formed a jogging team, rooted for each other, and gave out prizes for the best time.

The effects of the at-home peace movement were present, The love flowers painted on our new mess hall .We nicknamed our hooches. The nurses' hooches were protected by an eight-foot fence built by the Seabees. We called them Fort Chastity. The doctors' hooches were nestled together in a valley and called the Virgin Surgeon. There was a posting of signs to Los Angeles, Boston, New York, and Dallas with the mileage to each from Phu Bai—for instance, one read "St. Louis 29, 741"—just in case we wondered how far we were from our homes.

Nam gave me a legacy and a history. Nam was part of my path. I couldn't have not gone, and I am glad I did. If you went too, good for you.

Healing

Writing this book has been part of my healing process. My aim is to heal the wound that still festers and weeps, to get to the core and share my pain so the old wound can heal from within as it should.

I can no longer be invisible. Since attending the second national conference of service women in Boston in April 1988, I have realized that I must stand up and be counted. I must tell my story to those who will hear it and help my sisters who served, both in country and in hospitals in Hawaii, Japan, the Azores, and San Francisco during the Vietnam era. We all were together in the crisis—the nurses, Red Cross workers, stateside field hospital workers, and evacuation hospital personnel. No one came away unaffected, and we can only help each other. In a greater sense this little book is for all of us who left our comfortable homes to care for our fighting soldiers in Vietnam.

The Aftermath

I don't wait in lines anymore. Ever! I come back later or forget about whatever I was after in the first place. Having someone behind me makes me nervous. I don't trust what I can't see. If there is someone behind me, I move—once, twice, three times, whatever it takes to be free. I don't shop at any discount store where I cannot see the exit. I have a great fear of being trapped in a conflagration. I am hyperalert to sounds. I jump at loud noises and hit the deck at sudden explosions. A helicopter overhead quickens my heart rate and gives me goose bumps, as it makes me remember those medevacs and the series of events that followed once the copter touched down at the Twenty-Second Surg.

I always will remember.

Endings

Endings are difficult. I began this account claiming that the most tragic part of the story of women in Vietnam is that our story has gone untold, unrecognized, and for the most part, unknown. Now that you know the pain, longing, and sadness of a woman who has been in country and has come home, please don't forget us. I hope I have done my part by speaking out to stop the denial.

When history is denied and forgotten by society, it is bound to happen again. My only hope is that we will never again send our children off to some far-off place to fight in some dirty little war. The politicians created the war; let them put on their boots, and pick up their guns.

Yes, the truth may hurt, the truth may shock, but only the truth will set us free.

God bless you.

From one who served in Phu Bai, Vietnam
Lt. Bernadette J. Harrod, ANC

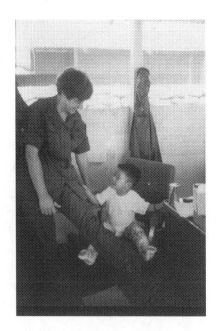

Favorite Things

What We Liked to Do Most

1. Set up a volleyball net and play, nurses against surgeons.
2. Set up jogging races to the perimeter and back, and try to beat our personal best times.
3. Send a tape recording home or, better still, listen to one we received from home.
4. Throw a small party in Graves Registration, when the place was empty. It was the only air-conditioned place on the compound.
5. Watch the war, when the flares went up at night.
6. Project the nightly movie on the side of the outhouse wall, and throw beer cans at it if it were bad. Most of the time, it was, whether it was *The Sound of Music* or *The Green Beret.* To make it interesting, we'd show the reels out of sequence and then try to figure out the plot.
7. Throw a barbecue party with beer and tunes, and dance under the stars and flares.
8. On very rare occasions, we would fly by chopper to China Beach; land on the sand; surf, sail, and swim all day; and go to a real officers' club for a sit-down dinner.
9. When we got a good spicy novel in a war pack, we'd cut it in three parts and share it with two other people. That way, three people could enjoy it at once.
10. Sit and listen to Mary play her guitar, and sing peace songs.

Favorite Songs

1. "We Gotta Get Out of This Place"—The Animals
2. "Leaving On A Jet Plane"—Peter, Paul, and Mary
3. "It's Much Too Nice a Day to Take a Life"

Favorite Novels

1. *The Prize*
2. *The Day of the Jackal*
3. *Hawaii*
4. *Caravans*
5. *The Word*
6. *Atlas Shrugged*
7. *War and Peace*
8. *Topaz*
9. *Airport*

Favorite Nam Talk in I Corps

1. What's happening?
2. When the going gets tough, the tough get going.
3. Don't sandbag me. (Don't tell me a line of bullshit.)
4. Don't mean nothing!
5. Airborne!
6. Phu Bai is all right!
7. 101st Airborne, the Screaming Eagles
8. Back in the world …
9. War is hell!
10. I am short, so short; don't tell me any long stories.
11. What's up, moose?

Things We Bought to Take Home

1. A Zippo lighter with a map of Vietnam and our company and corps logos on it.
2. A stereo, a Suzuki 5000, with receivers, reel-to-reel tape decks, and huge speakers.
3. Nikon cameras with very long lenses. Everyone became a shutterbug.

4. Extra poncho liners with camouflage designs to take to the beach.
5. Black silk jackets with maps of Nam embroidered on the backs. The colors were vivid.
6. Seiko watches for ten to fifteen dollars each. We sent one to everyone back home. We had never heard the brand name before and never thought they would become an expensive item.

Categories of Injured on Helicopters

Litters   categories were often expressed in numbers ie
                     2-5-3
Walking wounded   ie two litters, five walking wounded and three
                     expectants.
Expectants, meaning expecting to be prounounced dead

Letters Home

Letters were my way of staying connected to my family. I never knew that my dad dated and saved every one of my letters to Mom, my brothers, sisters, and aunts. Dad had been in heaven one year when my older brother, Charlie, found a folder in the attic titled "Letters from the War—Bernadette."

Thank you, Dad, for honoring our cause "to go where Uncle Sam needed us."

I am enclosing a few of these letters for you, dear reader, so that you can see how young, naïve, and patriotic we all were in 1969 in Phu Bai, Vietnam, as we tried to stop the spread of Communism.

Basic Training, Fort Sam, Houston, TX
February 1, 1969

Well, my combat boots are killing me, and this colonel is putting me to sleep talking about security clearance. Like I need to know this to pass a suture in an OR.

I am sitting in class now with combat boots and fatigues on. Check this out—we have to wear undershirts, and they have to show in the neck. Isn't that a scream? But you know, they feel good. The fatigues are so starched that my belly would be scratched to shreds without my XS olive-drab undershirt. Shit, my left boot is so tight, my foot has pins and needles. I feel bare with my hair all gone.

Well, my training is coming to an end. The days are long, 5:00 a.m. to 5:00 p.m. with marching, drill, classes, map reading, and a survival course.

Today we operated on a live goat. He was shot four times. The operations went well, but ours died of a heart attack.

It is hard to stand at attention when you have knock-knees.

Well, I have "one day and a wake up," and then I am off to Vietnam. I am scared. I would be lying if I said I wasn't. You know I love and miss you more than this pen and hand can tell.

Your loving daughter,
Bernadette

PS: Ya, we wear dog tags when we are in fatigues, so that's all the time for me. They are cold and noisy, but pleasantly comforting.

Bien Hoa, Vietnam
February 27, 1969

Well, greetings from sunny Vietnam. This letter will be short and sweet just to let ya'll in the US know that I arrived fine.

The flight was twenty-three hours long. Whew! My feet went from size 7 1/2 to 9D. We stopped after each five-hour block of flight time in Hawaii, Wake, Okinawa, and landed in Bien Hoa (near Saigon) only one hour ago. I was the only female with 164 men. I couldn't even light my own cigarette. They were great to me.

Now I am in an air-conditioned trailer under tight security in the Replacement Detachment 9375 in Bien Hoa, waiting to go to my permanent hospital. There is one first lieutenant nurse here who has been waiting for three days. So maybe I will be able to lounge here for a while.

There is the constant sound of helicopter and shooting.

It's the next day. My stay in the trailer was short lived—three hours. I am now in the female barracks with my little fan I got from Salvation Army (three dollars) in San Francisco. I still remain the only girl with two hundred guys. Complain—*no!*

I just got back from seeing the colonel, head nurse of all the hospitals here. I will be stationed in the Twenty-Second Surgical Hospital in Phu Bai. It is an inflatable MUST unit. Dad, call Lt. Col. Rogers at the Boston Army Base. She will send you some pictures and an explanation of the new MUST concept in a wartime hospital.

I will leave here sometime tonight—three to four in the morning to fly north. It is a three-hour helicopter flight. Loving every minute of it.

Love,
Bernadette

Bien Hoa, Vietnam
March 1, 1969

Dear Mom, Dad, Grace:

I am still waiting under fire in Bien Hoa. The average nurse spends twelve nights in the hunker due to firing around the base. My past two nights have been spent there. It's not bad, as we go to headquarters' bunker which is very large, and we poor females sleep on cots.

The firing is heard constantly in the distance. As a green first-tour second lieutenant, I always first think it is thunder.

You wouldn't believe all the kidding I take about my Boston accent. I am the only New Englander in three hundred guys. They crack up. Most of the guys call me Boston.

The Physical Therapist Captain is still here too. We have a good time together. She gets a kick out of me 'cause I don't know anything about the army way. She practices yoga every night. She is no phony either. She really gets into some weird positions. She can put both feet behind her head. Cool.

I don't know if I missed it or not. Happy anniversary, Mom and Dad.

I hate to ask for a care package so early, but straight off I found I needed certain things. Cough syrup, Vicks 44 preferably; nasal spray (any kind, two to three); all-cotton socks, high enough to wear [in] boots like Daddy's (two to three pairs); all-cotton bras (two), 36B, very little elastic. See, I am dying in these nylon bras, and they don't sell cold medicine in the PX, and you know I get at least three to four colds every year. The issue socks are too long, all the way to the knee, and they are 50 percent wool. You know how I hate wool anything.

So, hurry, please, Mom, these bras are killing me. Get cheap ones.

Hi, Grace. Hi, Tom.

No mail yet 'cause they send it to Phu Bai, and I stay here.

Love to all,
Bernie

PS: Ask the mailman about reduced rates for most mail going to Vietnam.

Phu Bai, Vietnam
March 4, 1969

Dear Mom and Dad:

Hurray! I have landed in Phu Bai.

The curtains need to cover a 32″ x 32″ square. In the door there is a top and bottom screen. Both are 32″ x 32″; so two separate curtains of the same material. This is my only source of natural lighting so choose the material with this in mind.

What the other nurses have done is to have their family sew up some curtain and string a heavy wire through top and bottom. Now, along the side of my house (hooch, or quarter of a hut) there are continuous screens. It is 24″ in height and 186″ long. You can make up some curtains for here too. The other kids have ones that are not all one piece; that is, they swing free at the bottom.

The above is a plea for CARE. I also need, right away: (1) ear plugs to quiet the bombing, (2) long-lasting candles with a small plate 'cause the electricity keeps going off. Tell Daph to take care of that as she knows all about candles. Help, I need a fly swatter. Also, you know they have these little kits with assorted screwdrivers, hammers, rulers. If you can find a cheap one, send that along too. It's not vital like the other stuff. I hate to sound demanding but I have to have the basic stuff of life. When there's a fly and nowhere to buy a swatter, it's tough.

Well, I finally made it up here to Phu Bai. It is right in the valley of a very pretty mountain range. The ground is totally pinkish fine sand, so it is dusty and hot or muddy and rainy.

I just got in last night so it is too early to tell you of the staff. They seem very nice so far.

I am not going to send my monthly check back to Boston, rather it will go to the Soldier's Combat Savings where it will earn 10 percent interest.

Bye for now. I will write later. Please do send me those things. Thank you. No mail yet; must be hung up in the country some place.

Your loving daughter,
Bernadette

Phu Bai, Vietnam

About the list of stuff I wanted you to send me: if you have not sent them yet, forget the cough syrup, as I got some here. But please do send me the other stuff, as I really need the items.

It's been cloudy and damp and cold since I have been here. There are no trees here—only sand or mud. The only nature [is] the rolling green hills in the distance.

Everyone here is so nice to me. It's a joy to wake up in the morning knowing that I am truly needed and respected.

That's all for now.

Love,
Bernie

Phu Bai, Vietnam
March 8, 1969

Dear Aunt Mary and Aunt Helen:

Hurray! I finally got a letter after three weeks, and you were the first. It was so great. The mail boy brought it over to me in the OR at six this evening. So, I am writing straight off to say, thanks.

Well, I am settling down here now after my week of being bounced around in Long Binh. I had my first full day OJT [on the job training]. We work twelve hours, then take call every night. But, there are three OR RNs, so one takes first call, second takes second, and the last third call. So, if there are only one or two casualties, the one on second and third may not be called in.

I will take call with my boss, Capt. Jane Jones, who is my hooch [room] mate. She is very nice to me. But she has a tape recorder that she plays endlessly. Please send some earplugs.

Also, my six pairs of undies I hung on the line yesterday are gone. Wouldn't that rot ya? Please send me three–four pairs, nylon, elastic leg, briefs—colored ones. They [the other RNs] say the Vietnamese steal them off the lines.

Last night we had a mass casualty—six shot-up Vietnamese soldiers. They were really badly off. It was a great experience. There are three–four teams of doctors so that they do two–three procedures on one patient at a time.

I loved the pictures of the snow. I showed them to the colonel chief nurse. She's the big cheese.

That's all for now.

Love always,
Bernadette

PS: It's very comfortable weather here. Not too hot yet!

Bai, Vietnam
APRIL 1969

Hi, Aunts:

I received a typewritten letter from both of you—thanks.

Thank you for the Saint Jude prayers. The snaps came intact. You are quite the packer. Thank you. I enjoy them so.

The sun is shining today so maybe the rains are over for this year.

No real news here except that I have settled in here nicely. Our club has a back room with a fireplace. At night we gather around the fire for old songs and a few drinks. War is hell.

It is so funny to take a shower with the insects. I don't mind bugs, but it is weird to swat down a few spiders before one showers.

All for now.

Lots of love,
Bernie

Phu Bai, Vietnam
March 24, 1969

Dear Folks:

I received your package of love this afternoon. It made me very sad because you care so much. Every little article was wrapped with love and affection. I could see Dad going through his precious tools to pick out a few for me. And you, Mom, whipping up a beautiful pair of curtains in an afternoon.

My cup runneth over now, for I am bursting with love for you, my parents.

When I first mentioned my coming over here I know you wanted to say no. But you didn't. That's what makes you such wonderful parents. You take your kids for what they are. Thank you for accepting my wild ways.

It's late now, and I have just finished stitching up our last GI for the night, I hope. I am soaked through to the skin with blood. It is caked on my shoes. I am spent.

This war is hell for the poor fighting man.

One boy died two times on the table but was resuscitated to wake up from the operation and give me a wink. I thought I would burst into tears.

The bombs are sounding loud in the background as I say goodnight to you, my loved ones.

All my love,
Bernadette

PS: In the letter I don't think I said thanks for the package. Thank you.

Phu Bai, Vietnam

Dear Mom:

The other day we had to shake down three female Vietnamese who work for the South Vietnamese radio station. [When I was] a kid, you know how I always wanted to be a rough, tough girl. Well, this was a dream come true. I had my own interrogation room.

We found two rolls of film and three maps. You see, some of these women are spies for the VC and work for Uncle Sam during the day.

After the shakedown, we had a buffet supper and drinks. Very nice group of officers there. I mentioned to the CO [head colonel] that we needed popcorn at the Twenty-Second Surgical. The next day at 1400 the chief nurse was delivered fifty lbs of kernels. She nearly died.

Please hurry and send the tapes so I can talk to you in the tapes of all my activities here in the war zone.

    All my love,
    Bernadette

Phu Bai, Vietnam DATES NOT NEEDED

I will sleep tonight with my bulletproof vest on and my helmet near my head. And thank God I wasn't like the three GIs we wheeled out the backdoor to Graves Registration.

A happier note is to follow in the a.m., but tonight I am so glad to be alive.

Your loving daughter,
Bernadette

SCARS & SCRAPES

The following pages are the first in what we hope will be a monthly newspaper for and by the personnel of the 67th Medical Group. In this inaugural issue, let us define what we hope this newspaper will be and what it will not be.

It is not a channel for official information; it will not contain directives or describe official policies from Headquarters. Such activity is better left to the 67th Daily Bulletin and staff letters. This newspaper is instead an opportunity for the members of the 67th Medical Group to talk informally about themselves, their units, and their activities.

Secondly, the *Scars and Scrapes* is not intended to serve as a fact sheet to the outside world, bragging about our activities. It is a family paper, intended primarily for the 1,709 men and women who make up [our] Group. Of course, we are not wholly self-centered: we hope you will send some copies home to your family and friends.

Thirdly, the newspaper is not a publication by Headquarters alone: it is not planned as a one street from Da Nang to points north and south. The present issue was mainly compiled by headquarters personnel: but we have merely taken the plunge in a trial run. The *Scars and Scrapes* is your newspaper, for all members of the 67th. In future issues we hope most articles will come from you, telling your fellow troops about what's happening at your hospital base of operations.

We need your comments, your contributions and your support. The Headquarters personnel have started the ball rolling; now it's your opportunity!

ZEALOUS JOGGERS, INCORPORATED, OF PHU BAI

LTC Donald Ellis, Commanding Officer of the 22nd Surgical Hospital in Phu Bai, has promoted and encourages participation in a physical fitness jogging program. LTC Al Graham, radiologist and runner nonpareil, was the "founding father" of Joggers, Incorporated. Twice a day, at 1100 hours and at 1600 hours, a hardy group of spartan doctors, nurses, MSCs, and enlisted men go trotting off on a one-mile circular course that runs along a road near the hospital. Each run usually last from 10 to 15 minutes, depending upon the physical condition of the respective runners. "One of your goals," relates MAJ Monroe "Mo" Levine, Chief of Professional Services, "is to finish the mile in eight minutes." LTC Ellis has noted that enthusiasm for the daily jogs has spread rapidly; every day the group grows larger as new members, who are determined to get in shape, join up. Many runners have acknowledged the healthy benefits derived from their grueling jogs. 2LT Bernadette J. Todesca [my maiden name]. Operating Room Nurse and former high school athlete, said that her sleep, appetite, waistline, and overall muscle tone have improved remarkably as a direct result of her jogging.

Phu Bai, Vietnam

Well, all is well here in downtown Phu Bai. We took eight 15-mm rockets last night. It was the first time Phu Bai was hit in ten months. Everywhere I go, I seem to draw Charlie [the enemy] with me. It's kind of exciting. I threw my bulletproof vest on and my helmet and crawled on my belly to the bunker.

Don't be frightened for me as the bunker is right outside my hooch, and we are heavily guarded by the men.

I put a second catch lock on my door (wouldn't want one of the horny GIs to get my beautiful bod). Hung the hook for my feather duster and fly swatter.

Now, the kitchen is saving me crates, which are rather soft wood so I can start to whittle.

Today I made a butterfly net out of an old mosquito net that the supply sergeant gave me. The butterflies here are beautiful so I hope to catch one. Please try to find a book on classifications of butterflies and how to mount them.

I practice my harmonica every day now. It's fun and, believe it or not, I think I may master it.

The guy Adam, whom I was telling you I liked so, caught malaria while at his three-week advanced [helicopter] training in Chu Lai. His best friend came over last night to tell me.

Well, his friend is just as nice, and we have a date.

I love my feather duster but it must have taken an awful beating in transit. She loses more feathers every day.

The supply sergeant gave [issued] me a huge Hunter rotating fan. It saved the day.

All for now!

Love,
Bernadette

Phu Bai, Vietnam

Dear Grace:

You could not believe the roar of these guns. I will never get used to them. At night the sky is ablaze with flares dropped from the planes to light the jungles so GIs can see the enemy.

Every night is the fourth of July. Easter came and went. A girl here gave everyone a molded cup with a flower on it. She's the flower child of the group. A real hippie but very deep and interesting to talk to.

Easter Sunday afternoon, Brad [a navy engineer] came by, and we went for a ride in an open jeep to see the bridge he built.

Oh, well, here's the check to cover the packages. Sorry I am so tardy.

All my love,
Bernie

PS: Camera is still in repair shop. I learned to play the Brahms's "Lullaby" on my harmonica.

Phu Bai, Vietnam

Yesterday we went to the beach. It was a beautiful outing. All the RNs piled into a "deuce & 1/2" [a big open truck with benches on the back]. We rode through Hue, got on a ferry, and arrived at the beach in Da Nang one hour later. The beach was an endless beauty of fine white sand, tall pines, and big waves. We bodysurfed, played keep-away, and thanked God for the escape of nature.

Sunday, I am off, and I have a helicopter ride up to the same beach. It's so cool to land the copter right on the beach.

War is hell, but Phu Bai is all right. On the serious side, we were mortared again this week. One shell hit a hooch down the road from us and blew it to hell. Luckily all the occupants had made it to the bunker in time. Adam is all better and back in his company now. But while he was away, I was going out with his best friend. Wow, what a mess!

That's all.

Love,
Bernadette

Phu Bai, Vietnam
April 27, 1969

Dear Folks:

I must tell you, although you must have heard by radio and TV, that the VC attacked our hospital at 10:00 p.m. on April 26, 1969. They fired four rockets,One landed on the medevac helicopter pad, demolishing one of the aircraft and deflating part of a medical holding ward and pre-op ward. You see, the sections of the bubbles are on separate air systems so that when a section is hit the whole ward doesn't collapse; just that section deflates.

The second rocket landed three feet from the chaplain's hooch. He is shaken up, but okay. The other rocket was a near miss on our ammo dump.

The fourth hit hard on the dust-off medevac helicopter compound doing lots of damage, but no casualties.

I know *Newsweek* and *Time* will blow this all out of proportion, because no one is supposed to fire on a hospital. Well, it happens in this dirty war. Luckily we had no casualties in our hospital compound, but there was a mass casualty on the perimeter and thus lots of business for the OR once the smoke had raised.

Yours truly was having a cool beer at the "O" club when they hit. With only eight weeks in country, I know what incoming rounds sound like. I hit the floor and [crawled] to the bunker. Everyone was safe and sound. We waited for the "all clear" signal, and Captain Jones and I went to the OR to pick up the pieces of the GIs that were hit …

It's 3:00 a.m. now, and my feet are caked with blood. I am weary and spent, scared and thankful.

Please don't worry about me too much. It's pure fate, and I am here 'cause the GIs need people with my background and training.

You know I love you all and miss you so much.

This letter is very different from my light and carefree usual notes. But there is the serious side to all wars.

Phu Bai, Vietnam

Dear Grace:

Life is fine here in Phu Bai. It's so hot, Grace. Don't ever complain about temperatures of 80–90°F. Think of poor old me here in Vietnam with 130°F tropical air. I have gotten so I sweaty, like Daddy does on those few hot days in August. It's really funny, Grace, when you think of it. A sweaty girl is probably the most unsexy thing in the whole world.

I still have an incurable crush on the chaplain's assistant. We now share a few words, and last night we sat next to each other at the movie. It's like puppy love.

We show nightly movies with a sheet on the bunker under the stars. It's really cool. A little different from the passion pits back in the United States, but "this is a war zone."

I am sitting here in the air-conditioned club (officers' club) with Stewart. He is a medevac. Very tall, thin, and very cute.

Phu Bai, Vietnam

Dear Aunt Helen and Aunt Mary:

Hi, Aunts. Glad to hear from you both so often. I really appreciate your continued correspondence. You don't know what it's like when I don't get mail. I even get a little paranoid.

Well, life is fine in Phu Bai. We continue to be very busy in the OR. Whoever says the war will end any day is unaware of the daily casualties.

Thank you for the spray of forsythia. It was a touch of spring.

The other day I went with the Red Cross girls to visit the men in the field. We went to three firebases and gave two programs at each base. It was so great to see these poor guys who are out in the boonies really fighting the war. I was so thankful for the luxuries of Phu Bai on returning.

Well, I fired a tank gun and an M16 and 155 Howitser mortar while out at the firebase.

God love the Red Cross girls, because I could never do their job. They present the same program eight times a day. We flew by copter from base to base, which is such fun.

The country is so beautiful. When the war is over, I would like to return and tour this place.

That's all for now—stay in good health.

Thinking of you.

Love,
Bernadette

Phu Bai, Vietnam

Dear Aunts:

We had a mass casualty yesterday and last night (thirty GIs to the OR). Very sad and hard work. We worked all day and night trying to save lives and limbs. Sad to say we had to amputate six legs. One GI lost both. I can't imagine how he can face life now.

Yes, my crush for Leo is God sent. In all this horror of war, he lightens my heart and makes me smile.

We [Leo and I] are going surfboard riding in Da Nang tomorrow. No need to wish for good weather for here; in Vietnam, it climbs to 130°F [each] day. Funny, huh?

Happy Mother's Day to my two second mothers. I would have sent you both a pretty card too but we were only allowed one per person, due to all the GIs and the rationed cards.

I am well and happy, so please don't worry.

A tape is in the mail in answer to the community one you sent me.

Love & lollipops,
Bernie

Phu Bai, Vietnam
May 18, 1969

Dear Aunt Helen and Aunt Mary:

Just a short note to let you know I am fine.

Received a note from you Aunt Helen with a clipping from a Boston paper. That's what I enjoy so—thank you.

We have been so busy the last five days doing twenty to thirty cases per day. I am on permanent nights until the fighting calms down. This month has flown by because it has been so busy. This push was later called Hamburger Hill.

Leo and I have been going up to the pool during the day. I am teaching him how to play tennis too. We really are enjoying one another. It's like a breath of spring in these tropics.

Read *Caravans* by Michener (author of *Hawaii*). The main character is a young girl who follows her heart's calling. I have now read all of his works and judge this [to be] his best.

So be good and remember me in your prayers.

Love always,
Bernadette

Phu Bai, Vietnam
August 18, 1969 FINE

Dear Loved Ones:

Hi, everyone! Here are few more photos for the hall of fame.

1. A fly-bye is the dust-off pilots' bye, bye for those people DEROSing or leaving. They fly the people that DEROS down to Da Nang. Once they take off, they circle and fly low over the helipad once more; the people on the ground throw colored smoke bombs. I was so pleased to catch this spectacular scene with my Instamatic.
2. Rose's sewing machine. It's a pedal job like Aunt Helen's. What a female can get in RVN [Republic of Vietnam] with "just a smile."
3. Picture of me ... taken by Dr. Welborn. I think it's awful.

Well, there is a tape on the way. Hope you got out to [my future in-laws, the] Harrods okay. It's a lovely idea.

The twenty-second is the new wedding date, but the paperwork is still not back. We are all due to leave the Twenty-Second Surg. on the twenty-third for our new duty stations.

So, God willing, we will be locked up here in Phu Bai.

The girls threw a shower for me. Oh, it was lovely! All details on tape.

Love you all so,
Bernie & Leo

PS: Send all mail to:
SP4 & 2 Lt. Leo Harrod
c/o Evac. Hospital
Chu Lai
APO 96325 San Fran

Phu Bai, Vietnam

Dear Folks:

All is well on the Eastern front. We are going through the myriads of paperwork to get married within the USA system. Will explain it all on next tape.

What I need from you folks is my baptismal certificate. Please send it right away by insured, registered, first-class airmail. We can't start the

papers through the chain of command until we "get our stuff together."
I have my birth certificate with me here.

Will send off tape soon. You know I love and miss you all so much,
especially during the upcoming marriage.

Your loving daughter,
Bernadette

Phu Bai, Vietnam
July /27, 1969

Dear Folks:

Hi! Hope you are all well. Guess what? I need my pastor's permission
to get married. So, please go down to see Fr. O'Rourke and get a letter
of permission to wed [and] get it in the mail quickly.

Before all this paper work gets straightened out, I may be ready to
come home.

Will write later. I love and miss you all very much.

Off to Da Nang to have a physical exam. Ugh!

Love always,
Bernadette

Phu Bai, Vietnam
July 11, 1969

Grace:

Hi, kid! Nice to hear from you again and again. You are too good to
write so often.

Please accept this check and a good luck kiss for your graduation.
Congratulations on a job well done. I am late for your graduation but
early for your birthday. That's me—all the way.

All is well in Phu Bai. Leo and I will be married in four to six weeks. August 15 is the date. Want to get me a short white gown and veil? What do you think? Father says you only get married once, and you should wear white. I could care less about all that white shit. It's so ticky-tacky. If you can get something cute, simple, and cheap, send it along. If it doesn't get here on time, it's okay. The dress is minor.

Happy Birthday!

Love,
Bernie

Phu Bai, Vietnam
July 28, 1969

Dear Loved Ones:

I just made you a long tape with reference to no mail for seven days. Well, it is 4:00 p.m. now, and I just received two from Aunt Helen and one from Aunt Mary, Grace, and Mom. I guess they were held up in country.

It was so great to know you are all well. I was so worried. I thought something had happened. Thank God you are all okay. Listen, if someone does get sick, contact the local Red Cross, and they will have me on a "Big Bird 707" and home in eight hours. God willing, this will never come to be.

Gee, Dad, I hope you are feeling better. I hate to think of you as getting old, but I guess that's it. "Don't let the bastards get you down." I love you, so I can't stand to think of you as unhappy. Now I am sad because you and I can't dance at the reception when they sing "Daddy's Little Girl." I love Leo very much, Dad. Too much to live in sin. You must try to understand why we can't wait until March '70 to be wed. It's selfish, yes, but we can't wait. Please be happy for us, Dad,

I miss everyone so much and certain ones at different times. Now I am crying over you, Daddy. Don't be so sad. You have been so good to us five kids. You gave us life, then years of love and devotion to …

turn [us] into respectable adults of society. Your gifts are many, Dad. Look around.

Please take this money, and go out to eat the night of my marriage. Be merry for I have found a man very much like my dear ole Dad.

I love you,
Bernadette

Chu Lai, Vietnam
January 30, 1970

Dear Aunt Mary and Aunt Helen:

Well, your package arrived today in excellent shape. It sure was a honey, full of good things to eat. The chocolate chip cookies were delicious. They are half gone already.

I am just now having tea with Donna [my friend], and we plan to have a grilled English muffin.

I have the pillowcases on and, boy, do they look nice. They add a little class and romance to this war-torn country. Thank you so much. I know a lot of love and time went into making them.

All is well here in Chu Lai. We [will] leave for Hong Kong and seven days of leisure after a long stretch of night duty. I received a tape from home, so we will be answering it before we leave for R & R, I hope.

I feel fine. My blood studies are okay. The doctor checked them out before I went on night duty.

We have started a square-dance gathering here at the hospital. Last night was our first lesson. Our caller is the supply sergeant. It was really fun.

Lots of love,
Leo & Bernadette
Married in Vietnam.
Amid a shower of rice, Specialist 4 Leo Harrod, USA, and his bride, the former Second Lieutenant Bernadette Todesca, leave the Hochmuth Chapel in Phu Bai, RVN. The bride is the daughter

of Mr. and Mrs. Charles J. Todesca of 50 Blanchard Boulevard, Braintree. The wedding took place on August 26. Both the bride and bridegroom are stationed at the 22nd Surgical Hospital in Phu Bai. Specialist Harrod, whose home is in Cincinnati, is the chaplain's assistant and his bride is a nurse at the hospital. (Official US Army Photo)

[Below caption was placed in newspaper image of original]

Romance Blooms for Army Nurse in Vietnam War

Sixty-five pages of documents and three postponements prefaced the wedding of Bernadette Todesca of Braintree and Leo Harrod of Cincinnati before their marriage could be consummated in Phu Bai, South Vietnam, where the bride was a Lieutenant in the Army Nurse Corps and the groom a Sp. IV and a Chaplain's assistant.

Now, legally wed with a license written in Korean to prove it, they are in the U.S. on leave. Following a visit to Hawaii, Hong Kong and to Leo's home en route, they are with "Bernie's parents in Braintree until April 18th when she will go to Fort Knox to serve out her enlistment. Leo having completed his tour of duty will attend Graduate School at Xavier University, Cincinnati, "only a hundred miles or so" from where his bride is based.

The course of true love is a rocky road in Vietnam because both civil and military authorities had to be placated; miles of red tape unwound; and a declaration of Leo's income verified before permission was given to post the banns for three weeks in the public square.

But … to put first things first, romance between the military is vitally concerned with protocol, even between Americans, when based in foreign lands. Another problem arose because Bernadette, a surgical nurse, outranked Leo, so the boy wooing girl technique had to be reversed. With Bernie, it was love at first sight and sensing that their interest was mutual, it was she who had to contrive situations to be together. Propinquity played the major role. Leo was the chaplain's assistant so Bernie became a regular attendant at chapel services and she always managed to sit close to the movie projector when Leo was the projectionist at shows for hospital personnel. By some lover's telepathy, the romance grew. In a war sector, opportunities for courtship are rare and now become the only measure of time. The dating process between an officer and a noncom is an obstacle course for the club of each is "off limits" for the other. By subterfuge, civilian disguises and hitchhiking with sympathetic pilot friends to remote bases where both were unknown, they managed, according to the age-old formula, "Love will find a way." A date was set, and the marriage was finally consummated on August 26, 1969.

The entire corps at the base went into action to make this a real wedding. It proved to be a reasonable facsimile thereof. The bride wore the only white dress within 50 miles, so it was borrowed for the occasion. Crowning her dark, close-cropped hair was a real Spanish mantilla. The Catholic chaplain, properly vestmented, provided an air of formality. Lt. Sue Cramer sang the Mass, accompanying herself on a guitar. Bernie's stand-in father, the pilot of a Chinook plane, gave the bride away. Because of the many postponements the male members of the wedding party had time to import formal attire from Hong Kong. The involvement of many creeds in the ceremony gave it an ecumenical aspect. For the reception Korean friends made the wedding cake; the Marines provided the champagne; and a pilot friend of Leo's flew the couple for a honeymoon in Saigon.

Since the 22nd Surgical Hospital where the two were stationed has been deactivated: with Leo discharged and Bernie reassigned, their future looks a little rosier than they dared hope. Anything will be better than the "hooch" in Fort Chastity, nurses quarters only 300 yards from the defensive perimeter of the base camp, where mortar and rocket attacks were no novelty; or the not much better quarters of their planned honeymoon home, a large boxlike structure that fits on the tail of a truck.

January 1971 when Bernie terminates her service with Uncle Sam is their target date for finding the home of their dreams.

Chu Lai, Vietnam
September 29, 1969

Dear Folks:

Hi, gang! Hope you are all well. I am sending you the negatives of the snaps that one of the guys [Mick] took with my camera at the wedding. We are going to keep the original prints because we have sent all the slides to you and Mom & Dad Harrod. We want a few prints to show our friends the gala occasion. Do get them printed up as they are really good in color and scope. They will make good wallet snaps for Mom, Dad, and [the] kids. Take the money for your set out of the $50 I sent home for shots. Okay?

We are pretty much settled in Chu Lai now. The one thing I really need is a bulb for my high-intensity lamp. It is a W-40 Westinghouse bulb. Daph knows, as she sent me one before. We only have the one overhead light, and it's bad because one of us can't stay up and read if he wants to, as it disturbs the other's sleep. So, save our marriage, and send the bulb. I have our sheets soaking in Axion tonight because Mama San does such a lousy job on sheets. Thanks for the Axion.

I got your letter, Grace, thank you.

Hope you got your last tape. We will wait for a reply and then send you off another.

My big fat major boss is okay. She is glad to have another in the OR, I think. It's awkward being the only girl with so many guys. They are as nice as can be, but it is unnatural.

The Harrods got the wedding album okay, so as soon as I show them to Neville, the girl who loaned me the white dress, I will send them on to you. We have two sets.

Tonight I made my first meal as Mrs. Harrod. We had pizza and beer. Leo has hit the hay, but I am not tired because I was off today and didn't wake up 'til the cows came home, or is it the water buffalo?

Tom, I hope you enjoyed your trip to Cincinnati. Do you think you will like calling that city home? Leo says that it is a lovely city. But nothing will be as good as Boston in my mind. But, I guess that's cuz Beantown is my forte.

This is getting to be a longie for me. But I guess you deserve it. I am sorry I didn't write for that long spell. Aunt Helen and Mary were really worried, and I wouldn't worry you all for the world. It's just that with the paperwork caper, the marriage, honeymoon, and the move to Chu Lai, we didn't have a minute to write, honest.

The Ninety-First is a rather big RA (regular army, hardcore) place. We have more lieutenant colonel major nurse types than we know what to do with. As a second lieutenant, I am nothing. The chief nurse has yet to have my introductory interview. That's how busy she thinks she is.

Tell me, did you ever get a duffle bag I sent from Fort Sam containing all my issued uniforms and extra clothes I had at basic? Do tell, cuz if not, you will have to write and make a claim to USA MFSS, Fort Sam Houston, San Antonio, Texas. I had at least a hundred dollars in civilian clothes in that bag, i.e., trench coat, two cocktail dresses, skirt, two blouses, and two pairs of shoes. The mail clerk said it would take two to three months to be shipped to Boston. But, as I have not heard a word from you, I now wonder if you ever got it.

Well, gang, I guess I had better shut off the light before Big Leo files for divorce.

We are very happily married and all. It's the only way to go. I only wish I had met Leo five years ago, but then again at that time he was "untouchable."

Bye for now. Thanks again for the nice letter, Mom. You are good correspondent and, Grace, you are too good to write so often when I never write you personally. I love and miss you all so very much during these happy days.

Love always,
Leo & Bernadette

PS: Please send the negatives to the Harrods when done. Thanks.

Chu Lai, Vietnam
October 6, 1969

Dear Mom, Dad, Grace, and Tom:

Hi, gang! How goes the battle? I want to thank you for the curtains. I didn't even have to iron them. I wired them up, and they make the hooch look like home. Thank you, Mother and Aunt Helen, for all the work and time that I know went into making them.

I am enclosing a check to cover the curtains and snapshot development. I know I told you to discontinue my checking account. Well, don't. I need the money to pay you for the stuff you send me. If you have closed the account, Mom, just draw out a sum from the savings account, please.

I know you must be tired of sending me packages and listening to me ask for stuff. I do so appreciate all you have done for me. Thank you. It's just for a little while longer folks.

All is well in Chu Lai. It has rained for eight days and nights. They had twenty-four inches in twenty-four hours in Phu Bai. I bet they were up to their behinds in mud.

I am on a five-night stretch. I have to stay in surgery, awake, for twelve hours—7:00 p.m. to 7:00 a.m. It's awful, and I hate it being away from Leo, but it's a "war zone."

Thanks for the note from you, Dad.

Grace, if you land that job it would be perfect. We will pray for you. Hang in there.

We hope to hear from you by tape soon. Lois Hurley is having her second child.

Lots of love,
Bernadette & Leo

PS: Look out for the wedding album as I did send it 6 October 1969.

Chu Lai, Vietnam
November 3, 1969

Dear Mom and Dad:

Because we have always been honest with one another, I know I have to tell you that I have infectious hepatitis. I have been in the hospital for three days now, wondering whether I should spare you the worry or level with you. Well, I feel that you have the right to know.

I will say don't worry, and I really mean it. As a nurse, I picked up my symptoms immediately and sought medical care. So, I was hospitalized immediately, tests confirmed my jaundice as hepatitis, and I was started on bed rest. Complete bed rest and increased fluid intake is the only treatment.

I feel tired and have no appetite for solids, but I tolerate liquids without nausea or vomiting. I am very comfortable here in the only air-conditioned ward [Recovery Room]. I have a lovely gatch [up-down] bed, radio, TV, and lots of good books, paint by numbers, and games to keep me occupied for my four- to six-week hospitalization.

Normally I would be evacuated to Saigon where RNs convalesce, but the administration is nice enough to retain me because of Leo. My poor Leo. I haven't exactly been my healthy, bouncing self since we wed. First the diarrhea; now this. He is the one that suffers. The poor guy. Honest, he is so good, patient, kind, and gentle.

At least we will be able to see one another even though we can't touch. God is really trying our love, but we accept his will and challenge. So, also I am asking you to accept God's will and not worry, please.

Your loving daughter,
Bernadette

Chu Lai, Vietnam
November 16, 1969

Dear Mom, Dad, Grace, and Tom:

Hi, folks! Well, another day of bed rest and another fifty MPCs [military payment certificates].

The doctor lets me out once a day now, so I sit by the sea and watch the waves gently roll over the rocks. Nature is so beautiful, especially when one is away for some time.

Leo was very touched by your letter, Mom. Thank you for thinking of him, as my illness has affected him so. I swear it is always harder on the well one when one of the two becomes ill.

I just love your card Grace. I got #1 okay, but the second one has me stumped. I am anxiously awaiting the answer.

I have been receiving cards from everyone, even Mrs. Sullivan, which was such a surprise. Do thank her for me.

Please tell me the balance of my checking account, and please do I pay a monthly charge for the checking account. Also, if my account is low, less than $200, please withdraw some from my savings account. Please, Mom, let me know about this, okay, as I need money for Xmas and R & R.

Today is my seventeenth day in hospital, and I am still the same. I have become quite good at crossword puzzles, reading fast, and praying.

The priest comes for communion and prayer, which is so lovely. You know me, I never sat still long enough to count my blessings. Well, during my stay, I have grown up a lot spiritually and emotionally.

There are three other girls in with me now. One is an Australian stripper with appendicitis; a major RN with back pain; and a lieutenant, also with back pain. I will be here when they are long gone.

As this is the ICU and Recovery Room, people are dying all the time, which makes it very interesting (clinically, that is). There is always something going on.

One of the nurses has some white bark chocolate (that white Fanny Farmer chocolate with almonds). She gave me a two-inch piece and, boy, I was homesick.

My yellow skin is fading, and the whites of my eyes are white in spots. Please don't worry about me. It's God's will, and he will take care of me.

Love to everyone,
Bernie

Chu Lai, Vietnam
October 31, 1969

Dear Folks:

I just got done talking with brother Tom via the Mars gram. The Mars calls are cheap, $2–$3, but very rudimentary. The signals from RVN go to a navy boat and are relayed to the USA. It has nothing to do with a satellite or Mars.

These calls must be placed … about eight hours before your call is put through. The service is offered to the bed patients. So when the man from Mars called the ward tonight, I asked if I could put a call through. Within four hours, I was talking to Tom.

As I told Tom, I had nothing to say. I just thought I would surprise you all. I think Tom could hear me better than I could hear him. Is that so, Tom? This poor reception is typical of Mars calls.

I was not at all disappointed to find only you in, Tom. I was thrilled to speak to my favorite little brother.

Well, just thought I would follow the call with the letter to explain how, why, and where I called from.

If I get the occasion, I will call again to say "I love you. Over."

Lots of love,
Bernadette & Leo

PS: Please address our mail as Mr. & Mrs. Sp. 4 Leo B. Harrod. Okay? My rank doesn't need to be on it, and Mr. comes before Mrs.

Chu Lai, Vietnam
November 21, 1969

Dearest Mom and Dad:

Just a quickie to tell you I am coming along fine. My blood studies have gone down to one-third of what they were at the peak. Therefore, the doctors say I will be out of the hospital in less than two weeks. Hurrah! There will still be weeks of being on quarters [no work], but at least I will be able to sleep in our own bed in peace and quiet.

Now that I am feeling well, this ward is getting to me. People dying, vomiting, crying, etc. It's not conducive to R & R.

I called Aunts Helen and Mary by Mars at 3:30 a.m., our time. I put my name on the list at 8:00 p.m., and that's when my call came through. I was thrilled to talk to them as the connection was excellent. I will try calling you folks the next time. We can only call once a week.

My paint by numbers is complete and looks quite good. With the extra paint, and an old small canvas, I am doing a modern art piece. You know how I love to dabble in modern art. Leo gets a big chuckle out of my attempts.

Thanks for all the get-well cards as they really keep me going.

Please go to the First National Bank, and get me cashier's checks from my savings account. Send as much as you can as I plan to spend that thousand on items in Hong Kong. You know, bedroom furniture, dining room set, etc. It's cheap there.

With the cashier's checks I can get travelers checks here at our American Express Bank. But my checking account in Boston is of no use to me in Hong Kong.

I hope you understand. And do get to this presently as I have no cash. The money in the soldier's savings can't be withdrawn. Please send the one or two cashier's checks insured, registered, etc. We plan to go to Hong Kong in the middle of January.

Our R & R came through for December 24 through January 2, so we will be away for both holidays. Great, huh? Just pray I will be all better by then. I hope so as it's a whole month away.

Happy Thanksgiving to you all.

Love and miss you,
Bernie

PS: Only my eyes are yellow now.

Chu Lai, Vietnam
December 3, 1969

Dear Mom, Dad, and Kids:

Hi! Here I am back in the hooch on one week of quarters [no work]. They will retake my blood test December 8 and then decide if I should return to work or remain on quarters until leave comes around on December 25. I don't care—I am just so happy to be back to Leo.

Today we made a whole side of one long tape, and it was incomprehensible. We were so disappointed. I think my tape recorder is on the blink or the tapes are old. They stick in the loaded reel and jerk off onto the take-up reel so that they pass sporadically over the recording heads. You "bic."

So, I have taken pen in hand to write you a decent letter. It is hard for me to write a letter in pain—only kidding.

I will call the bishop. If he can get down to see us, fine, but I am not tacking over the countryside to find some third cousin who means nothing to me. You can understand what I mean, I think.

Today Leo and I decorated our little tree. It looks almost real. All the bulbs are gold and one gold strip (garland). We got tinsel in the PX and did a real neat job of it. Thank you so much, Aunt Mary. We hung Santa over the kitchen. It and the tree are on a little red stand in the corner, so the whole scene hits you as you walk in the door. It's really quite effective (to use one of Mom's favorite words).

Well, we just had a ball making the place look like Christmas. We hung the Christmas basket from the lamp.

The little candle I light at mealtime, cuz, I guess, I am one of the last of the true romantics.

Thank you all for the cards and many notes and letters of cheer while I served my time in the hospitals—thirty-two days is a long time to be on one's back, and the separation from Leo was hell. I can't believe you ate out for Thanksgiving. You deserve the rest, Mom, but I hope Dad wasn't disappointed in the restaurant's meal.

Don't worry about Tom. It's an awful age. I am sure he is fine, and a big hug and kisses from me would straighten him right out. Well, we will enjoy your nut loaf. It arrived in good condition, Mom, and the soup is already gone. Thank you so much.

The rainy season continues with an occasional (one in every seven) day of sunshine.

Send no more food as we are overstocked and will do well to finish off those canned goods before we leave, you "bic."

Hope your eyes are okay. Take care of yourself. Don't let the bastards get you down.

Grace, hope your cold or tired blood or whatever is better. Keep cool.

That's all for now. Sorry about the tape. Send us one on a new one, okay. I think ours are all too damp and sticky.

All our love,
Leo & Bernadette

PS: Tried to call you, but no one was home.

Chu Lai, Vietnam
December 22, 1969

Dear Mom, Dad, and Kids:

Just a quickie while the patients are eating. I got the check from Margie okay. Thank you.

Leo and I are getting packed for our R & R. We are so excited, it will be like a second honeymoon.

I am feeling great. My liver function studies are A-OK. Have been doing head nursing on the quietest ward in the hospital. I really love it. Been practicing to speak the language. It's fun.

We are going to a Mass by Cardinal Terrence Cook [of New York; he succeeded Cardinal Spellman] at 4:00 p.m. today in the amphitheater.

We will miss Bob Hope as he comes to Chu Lai on the twenty-fifth. Do see it on TV, though, so you can visualize how beautiful RVN really is.

I must get back to my charges. A very happy and blessed New Year to all my family in Braintree.

Love to all,
Leo & Bernadette

Cam Rahn Bay, Vietnam
December 25, 1969

Dear Folks:

It's Christmas Day, and Leo and I are having coffee in the USO at Cam Rahn Bay awaiting our 3:00 p.m. flight to Australia.

We came down by the medevacuation plane that the air force runs. We were the only well passengers, as all the others were sick and wounded GIs. It was interesting to see how they stack the letter cases (three high).

The flight was the smoothest we have had in country. We were so happy that they let us spend the night together. We were not expecting this treatment, and we were willing to stay up all night. But when I checked into the BOQ Bachelors Officers Quarters, the sergeant said that the commanding officer lets married EMs and officers share the BOQ rooms.

Our room was very nice for Vietnam. Complete with fan and night light.

On Christmas Eve we went to a combined Catholic/Protestant candlelight service at 7:00 p.m. There were two ministers and one priest. Afterward, we went to the officers' club where they had a band.

This morning we went to a real nice Mass. It is so moving to hear all men's voices sing carols. Leo has a lovely voice, which nicely drowns mine out.

The flight to Sydney is twelve hours, with a stop in Darwin to refuel.

Cam Rahn Bay is a flat, sandy are with rolling sand dunes and scrub pines. The mountains are seen in the distance.

We have two days in-country travel time when we come back, so we will rest up here before we return to Chu Lai.

It seemed so funny to be away from Christmas. I knew it was December 25, but the war and army don't stop for the holiday. Going to church helped to remind us, and we carried the spirit of Christmas in our hearts.

I hope Christmas at 50 Blanchard is the same hustle-bustle happy time. I wish you all the very best Christmas.

In the USO(programs for the down times the soldiers may have) here, they have big green tree and a train under the tree. It is very nice to be setting here with my love on Christ's birthday.

Both Leo and I feel so sorry for all the lonely GIs. Their faces look sad and blank. Oh, some get drunk to try to escape, but the loneliness is still there.

I get mad when I think about all those hippie demonstrators and then look at these poor GIs.

Well, folks, Leo and I wish you the best in 1970.

All our love,
Leo & Bernadette

Chu Lai, Vietnam
February 8, 1970

Dear Aunt Helen and Aunt Mary:

Hi! Hope you are both fine. This is just a line to tell you that Big Leo and I are safe and sound back in Vietnam. Or as safe and sound as one can be in RVN. Our vacation was like a dreamland. I would never think of Hong Kong for a vacation spot, but it really is a quaint, beauty of a spot. We have one month more to work, then freedom. So, have your teakettle steaming, cuz Leo and I will be there for tea with the aunts.

I will tape you about the trip. We are well and hope you are too.

Lots of love,
Leo & Bernadette

Chu Lai, Vietnam
January 27, 1970

Dear Mom, Dad, Grace, and Tom:

Hi, folks! Hope you are all fine! We are getting short—forty-three days left in Chu Lai. I don't have to tell you how anxious we are to get back to the "the world."

I am working nights (eight straight) before we go on leave. I like working nights cuz I am my own boss.

I just want to tell you that my orders came down on my birthday. I have to report on April 22 to Fort Knox, KY, Ireland General Hospital. It was one of my three choices and pretty close to Leo.

So we will have a long vacation before I have to report. We still plan to drive cross-country and see the beautiful West on our way home.

We will stay with Mare and Phil a few days and then rent or drive a car out for someone wishing their car to be in Ohio. You know what I mean.

We leave for Hong Kong February 2, so we should be out of RVN for holiday, I hope it isn't much this year.

All is well with us. We remain very happy in love despite all this war. We shipped our hold baggage [two trunks] home to Ohio. So we are all ready to leave March 14.

Grace, I got your letter today and glad you understand.

Love,
Leo & Bernadette

Chu Lai, Vietnam
January 21, 1970

Dear Mom, Dad, Grace, and Tom:

Hello! Hope you are all well. I have received two letters from you, Mom, that we have enjoyed. Thank you. My letter writing has gone to pot.

We have fifty-one days to go yet, and boy are we anxious to put our feet on US soil.

I am back on nights and enjoying being out of the OR for good.

See you soon,
Leo & Bernadette

Chu Lai, Vietnam
March 2, 1970

Dear Mom & Dad:

Hi! Well, I did it again—I missed your anniversary. I am very sorry, but I guess you know how "sorry" I am. Please accept this gift from Leo and me, and use it in the best of health.

We ordered your china. It's a service for eight in white wild rose in yellow by Sanyo of China. It's very pretty, and I am sure you will like it. We hope so anyway.

We are getting so-o-o-o short—I can't fill normal-size notepaper anymore.

Thank you for your most recent letter, Dad. I always enjoy hearing from you. We are busy now clearing post and packing.

Dad Harrod had a gallbladder operation after an acute attack at work. He is okay now but sore. We received a tape from Mom Harrod explaining all the events.

Say hi to the aunts for me. I must drop them a note.

Call Daphne and tell her I got her Nikon but will have to hand carry it home as Nikon products can't be imported to the US. It cost $155 with a built-in through lens, automatic light meter. Lens 35mm with hard leather case.

Love to all,
Leo & Bernadette

PS: Please cancel my checking account.

Poems

By Bernadette Harrod

A Voice

I will not be silenced any longer
You cannot put a Band-Aid on my gaping wound and call me better
Where were you twenty years ago when I came home?
Your guilt and your shame for leaving us forgotten
Tastes like a bitter herb under my tongue
I will not go stand in a corner
I will run to the highest mountain and shout my story
Loud and clear!

Life and Limb Saving

Where do you go to
Wash away the blood
Where do you go to forget the horror
The mud
The blood
The bugs
The heat
The endless line of battle wounded

We do our best
We patch them up
Remove their shattered, splintered limbs
And send them back
To where
To what

Oh! Where have they gone to—
From my first stop—
Along the way—life and limb saving

Are You Ready?

Are you ready to hear about the evil of Vietnam
Babies shot in a crossfire
Napalm bombs planted on our own sergeants by their own boys

Are you ready to view the sure, realistic horror
Top sergeants shot between the eyes in a friendly unit card game
A female Red Cross worker brutally stabbed by a GI

Are you ready to hear more, or do you just want to hear that
Yes, we were there, and yes, we were proud to be there
Oh! Okay, put on your blinders
Let the time go by and you too will be sending your children off
To a faraway country to share in a new Holocaust

Trust

Even now, I don't trust—especially people
I question their sincerity
How genuine are their glib comments on Vietnam
"Oh, that must have been interesting"
That's the red flag—balloons go up
Say no more
Shut up, cuz they really couldn't care less

Never

Ya, Uncle Zake went to the war
    Four year, Ayuh!

But he don't talk none about it
Ayuh!
Zake walks funny
Shrapnel in his hip, ayuh!
Never complains
Old Zake
Funny old koot
Likes his own company, ayuh!
Never did get married
Fancies a drink, though
Ain't it funny how he never talks about it
Never! Ayuh!

Forever Nineteen

Did you really think this was going to be the last war?
Did you feel proud when the final bullet leveled you to the ground?
Did you hear the pipes playing and the drums roll?
You probably never even wed or fell in love for sure

You never made it to you parent's twenty-fifth wedding anniversary
Has anybody called you uncle yet, or dad?
Your life was leveled, cut off at the waist
Perhaps below the waist

Did you look back as your torso fell to the ground?
Wondering, will anybody know I was here?
That I fought and was killed
Gone at nineteen!
I will never forget you, for I cared for you
I bandaged your stumps and yelled into your face
Soldier! Son! But you were gone at nineteen

How I try to forget you, the ones who were gone on arrival
How I tie up my running shoes and run and run to forget your face
But you are always right around the corner

The face with the eyes that would not open
Some mother's little boy
Gone at nineteen!

Uncle Bud Was in the War, but He Never Talked about It

Sure, Uncle Bud was in the war, the big one, WWII
The German officer's hat—he sent it home by mail
What did he do with the German officer?

For years I would play war with the hat on my head
And my Annie Oakley guns—one on each hip

Uncle Bud would come to visit
I wanted to ask him about the war and about the hat
"No, no!" Mother would say. "Bud doesn't talk about being overseas"

Twice a year Uncle Bud would come home alone
Hat in hand to visit
Never took off his coat—hat in hand

He had the saddest eyes
And he sat like a soldier on the edge of the Queen Anne chair
Ready to retreat at a moment's notice

"How are you, Gertrude?" he would always ask
And Mom would chat on and on
"What about the war, the heat, and your sad eyes, Uncle Bud?"
But silent I would sit by my mom's feet and stare up at Uncle Bud

"I must be going now, Gert"
Heart in hand and a kiss on the cheek
Off Uncle Bud would go 'til Christmas

Christmas and Easter, he would come to call
Hat in hand

Completing the Circle

Twenty years' battle—five old souls
Gather around a table in a VA hospital
Trying to complete the circle
Sharing our pain, our quiet, and our remorse
Finding the answers—
Why we went?
What we did there?
How it affected our lives forever
Five old souls, twenty years later
Begin to peel back the onion, layer by layer
Some of us weep
Revealing our most traumatic moments
Sharing how we built walls to block the pain and sorrow
Twenty years later we gather together
To take down those walls, brick by brick
Let out the pain, and let in the sunshine of hope and pride!

A Call from the Lowell Sun

Just when I had put Nam on the shelf, way up high
So that it couldn't wake me up in the middle of the night
Just when I had become honest with myself
Stopped the drugs to dull the pain
Just when I could watch veterans parades and
Turn on the TV on November 11
I get a call …
This is the *Lowell Sun*
A young voice wants to know
What was it like?
Why did you go?
What did you do?
What was it like to come home?
Do you watch *China Beach*?
The hairs on my forearms stand straight up

In an instant I am defensive, angry, and want to shout
Fuck you, asshole!
You will never know, you pubescent yuppie
Do Holocaust victims rent videos about Treblinka?
Do Korean vets watch reruns of *MASH*?
Do Vietnam veterans hang on to *China Beach*?
We think not!
We try to do the best we can with what is left
A life pulled into perspective
Some of the sorrow is gone
But with it went some of the joy
Some of the horror has lessened
But with it went some of the love
The memories have faded from 3-D Technicolor
To muted tones and halftones of grays and purples
But they do come back to haunt you
Especially when you get a call from the *Lowell Sun*

It Won't Be Over 'Til They Are All Home

How many are missing?
It's not over yet!
Every Veterans Day isn't a real celebration
Our boys are still behind enemy lines
Lost in Nam; their poor mothers

If Sly Stallone would lead a real group
I'd gather some nurses up and
We would dust off and bomb away
Drag our boys out of that land
And bring them home

Then and only then can we rest and close the door
On that page of history
I can't understand why we can't negotiate
For those POWs and MIAs

Give the Russians whatever they want
Subs, planes, wheat, grain, violins, anything
A human life has no price tag
Our warriors were left behind, and
Forgotten!

Under the Microscope

Twenty years later a rare species is discovered:
Those who served in Vietnam
"Did you know nurses were there?"
"Let's call them up and ask them why"

Twenty years later they want to smear us on a slide
And study us
"I will not be under a microscope," part of me cries out
But how will we learn to isolate the virus of war
Military advisory, or
Police actions?
How can we prevent the spread of this
To an all out "era"?

Dirty little wars fester into all-out Holocausts
And unless we go under the microscope and tell
How and when it happened
Vietnam will happen again
Like an undetected virus
It will affect another land in another era
And young men and brave women
Will hear the sound of distant drums
And march into a known horror
To defend our rights in distant lands.

Under the Anger

You're an angry Vietnam Vet
You bet your ass I am!
I have every right
But beneath the anger, fury, and rage
Sits a pool of sadness so deep
Filled with unmentioned bodies that swell and bloat and come to surface
Unmentioned bodies of killings, torturing, babies dead in utero.
Practicing on the enemy
"Hero, let me saw the gook's leg off"
"Don't waste any good suture on that VC"
"Anybody want to practice intubating?"
"I do; he's just a gook"
So I learn skills outside my practice
Skills I will never use back in the world
Oh, I could cut your leg off to save your life
Or, intubate if you died
But there's not a lot of call for that in Natick, MA
That was in the bush in Nam
And this is in the world.

The Last Pair of Round Eyes

Hey, round eyes, what's happening?
Don't mean nothing
Hey, round eyes, where you going?
To work, GI, to the OR
"Oh," he says, knowing his shot-up buddies come to my place
The OR doors swing open
I am all set
My instruments are all laid out
Alices, kelleys, lap pads, by the fifties
Two or three saws to cut off your crushed and splintered limbs.
Protected from you behind my mask
Gloved, I break, scrub

To come to you
You're only eighteen, a blue-eyed son of some proud mom
I go for your hand, we clutch one another
You go for my eyes
"Hi, round eyes"
"Hi soldier, you're okay
We got you now; you're in good hands"
A smile or perhaps a wink form over the drapes
I say hello and good-bye
I'm your last stop
A refuge in hell
The last thing you remember are my brown round eyes.

Phu Bai, Vietnam

Who of you, has worn my
boots
or felt my pain?
Who of you
has seen my sweat

or felt my fear?
Only those who have
walked in my jungle boots,
felt my fatigue,
and cried similar tears
will ever know
the deep wound of Vietnam—
of seeing young men
blown away.
Double,
triple
amputees;
chest wounds;
head wounds;
multiple frags;
the never-ending line
of ORs.
The human bloodbath of
Hamburger Hill and
the Tet Offensive.
But worse than that
horror
is the emptiness of
coming home to
ungrateful hearts
who asked us
why we served,
why we went
over there anyway.

Twenty years later
we gather together,
those who served.
We wonder,
reflect, how has it
changed our lives?

For me,
Nam made a difference.
I'm a little bit stronger and
a lot more patient.
I value a sunset as much
as a Big Mac.
I don't take my freedom
for granted.
I cry at parades when
cub scouts march
in front of the old vets.

And I remember
Vietnam.
I always will.
When a Huey
flies overhead,
floods of memories
come to me of
Phu Bai and the Twenty-Second Surgical.
And I remember.

A Soldier Doesn't Need a Thank You

When you lay down your life
on a battlefield,
or leave two arms and one leg
behind you in the bush,
there is no thank-you
big enough.
So don't bother.
When you forget the parade down Fifth Avenue,
don't bother
with lesser attributes
on state house grounds,
Too little, too late …

You're slapping a
Band-Aid on an open wound
hemorrhaging and pulsating,
Rotten, deep to the bone.
A wound the nation failed
to tend, and it went rancid,
and the limb was severed
at the hip.
So save your watered-down
fizzless speeches,
your ten-minute
spots on national news.
We don't need your publicity, or recognition.
You can't thank a patriot.
A war hero's enkindled
from within.
You can't understand
why she went,
and you can't
thank her for going.
She went because
she had to.

CAPE COD 2007

Even Now

Even now,
after twenty years,
I still feel
abandoned and forgotten,
uncounted,
unnumbered.
Left to change all alone
in an airport ladies room.
"You go over there."
Go to the corner and wash
the mud and the blood.
Forgotten, silenced, and cast away
for over two decades
and now I can't deal with
the newly kindled interest:
"Did you see '60 Minutes'?"
I want to scream and
rip off their faces.
Where was your interest
and empathy over the past
twenty years?
Buried out back,
with your old, dead dog?
You didn't give a shit in "69,
and you could care less now.

Alone

A single female
Alone, I walk
Into an unknown
Alone, I went
Alone, I returned
And, alone, I remember

How it was
For me ... over there

Knowing

I have to know you are out there, and you care
I have to know you remember me, and I made a difference
The circle has gone on for so long, unfinished.
Does anyone know where Phu Bai even was?
I haven't a name or a clue where you all
went, or what has happened to you
Are you happy we saved your lives? Was it enough?
Can you function without the two legs we buried in the dirt in Phu Bai?
Did they ever close your colostomy?
Did your liver laceration seal itself off?
Where are you all now, twenty-five years later?
I have to hear from one or two of you soon
It's lonely in the wondering!

If I Write It

If I write it, it will not own me
If I get it out there, then it's mine
My name will be on the front cover and a picture on the back
The country tried so hard to forget Vietnam
Sometimes I question if I was ever there
But if I write it, then you'll all know of the horror,
The mayhem and the killings of village mothers and unborn babies
Of friendly fire and crossfire accidents
Of times when GIs died because we didn't have enough sutures
Of the human strength to save them all

We did the best we could, we were only girls at best
New to the field—young nurses—new officers
Strangers in an alien horror

The endless stream of broken, screaming bodies
Peal a buddy off his wounded friend
"He'll be okay, he's in good hands"
How many times did I say those lies?
The good hands of the surgeon couldn't save him
And he slipped away with the smile of anesthesia on his face

How many did we treat?
How many limbs did I saw off?
Countless blue-eyed babies, some mother's child of eighteen
Gone to stop the Commie pigs
Charlie shot him down
And I tried to save him
Lies, lies, lies
My country told me lies
And, if I write it down, it becomes truth again
Yes, I was there
Yes, I was part of it
And, yes, I came home

When I Was Young

When I was young, I wanted to be a cowgirl
and shoot the bad guys dead
To ride into town with a big white hat and silver guns, one on each hip
"There she is," the silent, awestruck crowds
would whisper one to another
Now that I'm older, I realize I'm scared to death of horses
And there ain't no bad guys, and there ain't no good guys
Just shades of mediocrity
My silver gun rests on a shelf
Way up high in my little boy's closet
"Oh, those are Mommy's guns," he'll say
And as for the glory, there is little
Cuz you see, I grew up to be nurse, not a cowgirl, after all

But nurses wear white hats and walk in
glory to heal the broken bad guys
It was a good and honest childhood dream,
and I got a lot of miles out of it
For what is childhood except to dream and wish of what's to be.

Wasted Words

Listen to the whisper of the dying masses
Rattling like empty trash cans
Blowing up the street on a windy day
Why do people talk so much?
Would a little silence kill them?
Does the wind on the sill make them so nervous
That they have to fill every walking moment with mindless chatter.
About
this one
that one
this thing
that thing
Take me on a winged dove to live with the polar bears
Who haven't wasted one breath on a single phonic sound.
Let me live among the penguins.
We could hop around and dive off icebergs into the frozen brine.
And dry ourselves in the wind and hear the wonderful silence
Of the north winds.

Pain

Pain is the touchstone of all spiritual progress
It is the root of all growth
Because when I get to the depths of my pain
There is no place to go but upward
Losses, piled deep
Losses on top of lasses

Lost loves
Broken marriages
Old loss of unsung
War heroes made to stand in veterans hospitals
Waiting lines to be seen for battle wounds
That still fester and burn deep in their soul
New losses of old ways of dealing with life
Take a drink is dead for good, and I mourn that loss daily
New, and old, half forgotten,
All my losses gang up on me, and I mourn them
All at once in a deep-felt depression of dark sadness and never-ending
gloom
If I were an Indian, I would go to my teepee and light a small fire
And stay there until the Season of the Big Leaves comes
Because my father has gone, and I need the time and the freedom to
grieve
and wail and mourn
As the American indian
did when their fathers died
I'd hibernate and talk to my spirit guide
I'd paint my face with dark pigments
Sit cross-legged and throw some incense into the open flame
I'd sit until what white men call spring arrives
Then I'd come slowly from my grief tent and
welcome the new life once again

Weary Wars

I am tired of the battle
It excites me not
The battleground has grown old
And your weapons of hurt and neglect and name calling
Don't hold their old sting
Let's lay down our arms of hurt and blame
And let the horses smell the victory and graze upon the grass
You can retreat to your front

And I can rest on my lands
Let's not war about the neutral zone
Haven't you had enough?

Those Who Serve

They also served, a league of caring souls,
who left their homes, their comfort
to go to a far-off place,
to fight in a dirty little war.
For who has worn my boots
or knows the cries or felt my tears,
sensed the dread of death and dismembered bodies,
bloodied bodies on top of bloodied bodies,
six litters, followed by walking wounded.
Triage the ones we can save,
twelve-hour days in an operating room, six days a week.
And who cares?
Who knew who we even are?
They didn't even count us as having been there.
Twenty years hence, interest is rekindled.
War is romanticized.
And they ask,
Why did you go?
What was it like?
How did you cope?
Too little, too late to really care.
Your question comes twenty years too late.
Your current interest is lost in all the years of silence and envy.

IS   NOT FREE

B.J. Harrod
2010

Army Hospitals in Vietnam

FOR THOSE THAT SERVED IN THESE HOSPITALS, THIS IS A REFERENCE OF DATE, LOCATION AND NAMES OF HOSPITALS.

Hospitals	Dates	Location
Second Surgical Hospital	7/66 to 4/67	Qui Nhon
	4/67 to 1968	Chu Lai
	1968 to 4/70	Lai Khe
Third Field Hospital	5/65 to 12/72	Saigon
Third Surgical Hospital	9/65 to 5/67	Bien Hoa
	5/67 to 9/69	Dong Tam
	9/69 to 4/72	Binh Thuy
Sixth Convalescent Hospital	5/66 to 6/71	Cam Rahn Bay
Seventh Surgical Hospital	8/66 to 4/67	Cu Chi
	4/67 to 1968	Long Giao
Eighth Field Hospital	4/62 to 9/70	Nha Trang
	9/70 to 1971	An Khe
	1971 to 8/71	Tuy Hoa
Ninth Field Hospital	7/65 to 9/68	Nha Trang
Twelfth Evacuation	12/66 to 12/70	Cu Chi
Seventeenth Field Hospital	4/66 to 3/68	Saigon/Cholon
	3/68 to 7/69	An Khe
	7/69 to 10/69	Qui Nhon
	10/69 to 8/70	An Khe
Eighteenth Surgical Hospital	7/66 to 12/67	Pleiku
	12/67 to 2/68	Lai Khe
	2/68 to 3/69	Quang Tri
	3/69 to 12/69	Camp Evans (Gia Le)
	12/69 to 8/71	Quang Tri
Twenty-Second Surgical Hospital	3/68 to 10/69	Phu Bai
Twenty-Fourth Evacuation	1/67 to 11/72	Long Binh
Twenty-Seventh Surgical Hospital	4/68 to 6/71	Chu Lai
Twenty-Ninth Evacuation	8/68 to 10/69	Can Tho/Binh Thuy

Thirty-Sixth Evacuation	3/66 to 11/69	Vung Tau
Forty-Fifth Surgical Hospital	11/66 to 10/70	Tay Ninh
Sixty-Seventh Evacuation	10/66 to 1972	Qui Nhon
	1972 to 1972	Pleiku

Navy/Marine Corps Hospitals in Vietnam

Hospitals	Dates
Da Nang Naval Hospital	1966 to 1970
USS *Repose*	1966 to 1970
USS *Sanctuary*	1966 to 1971
First Marine Medical Battalion (First Division)	1966 to 1970
Third Marine Medical Battalion (Third Division)	1965 to 1969

Support/Evacuation Hospitals	
Naval Hospital	Okinawa
Camp Butler	Okinawa
Guam Naval Hospital	Guam
Okinawa	
Okinawa	
Guam	

Air Force Hospitals in Vietnam

Location	Dates
Bien Hoa AB	1965 to 1972
Binh Thuy AB	1966 to 1970
Cam Rahn Bay	1965 to 1972
Da Nang	1965 to 1972
Nha Trang	1962 to 1969
Phan Rang AB	1966 to 1972
Phu Cat	1967 to 1971
Pleiku AB	1966 to 1967
Tan Son Nhut	1962 to 1973
Tuy Hoa	1966 to 1970

Support/Evacuation Hospitals	
Kadena Air Force Base	Okinawa
Tachikawa Air Force Base	Japan
Clark Air Force Base	Philippines
Hickman Air Force Base	Hawaii

Issues and Concerns of Female Vietnam Veterans

- admitting one's own "delayed stress" is a threat to one's professional reputation
- various levels of denial
- numbing over of feelings
- amnesia about much of the Vietnam experience
- aloneness and isolation
- retaining only selective memories
- gender identity problems
- sexual issues
- short-term, intense relationships in Vietnam making it difficult now to establish good, long term relationships
- sexual dysfunction due to depression or other sequellae of Vietnam
- trauma versus trivia: being able to handle major crises but having little patience for minor problems
- shame and guilt over being a Vietnam veteran and about things done or attitudes expressed in Vietnam
- no sense of identity with other Vietnam veterans or inability to feel like a veteran
- depression and a sense that life has no meaning
- fears of rejection by society and other veterans
- avoidance of connecting with own fear of mortality
- lack of self-esteem or self-value
- sense of unfinished business in Vietnam
- anger and rage
- free-floating anxiety
- sleep disturbances
- lack of validation, feelings that "I don't have the right to feel this bad"

- alcohol or drug abuse
- emotions concerning being a minority person
- family system affected by delayed stress
- self-punishment, leading to slow suicide
- possible residual effects from sexual harassment in the military
- "action junkie"—trying to recreate the adrenalin high of Vietnam
- the need to be in control all the time, which leads to the fear of losing control or inability to keep emotions in check
- self-perception as helper, which leads to difficulty in asking for help even from a therapist

Appendices

The appendixes consist of articles about me, the group therapies I sought out and attended, and the dedication of the nurses' statue. The statue honors not only the registered nurses but all the women who served their country during the Vietnam War. There is also a monument for all the women who served their country; the Women's Memorial," as it is called, sits at the entrance of the Arlington National Cemetery. The memorial has a computer database where you can tell your story and include pictures of yourself while in the service and today.

I also track my personal recovery by telling my story both inward and outward. My personal healing began at the first conference of Women in the Military hosted by the Joiner Center at UMass Boston. There, I finally met people who could and would help me with my PTSD. Jessica Wolf formed the first support group for nurses who served in Vietnam. We met every week for over one year. Each session validated my postwar trauma. Nurses talked about needing to function as the first assistant to the surgeon, which is normally a physician's role. We also performed operations outside nursing practice, e.g., amputations, debridement, and clamping and tying off bleeders.

The Framingham Veteran Center in Massachusetts is a place where all veterans can receive therapy and find support groups. Maggie Dodd ran and held medical support groups. She was instrumental in my healing. Included in these groups were nurses, medics, combat veterans, and medical service personnel. They were all mixed together in the groups for their support and healing.

In 1984, the Vietnam Memorial Project was started by a few brave souls. It was discovered through this program that eleven thousand female military personnel were stationed in Vietnam. Eight thousand of those women were registered nurses. Eight military nurses were killed, and their names had been placed on the wall at the Vietnam Veterans Memorial. Approximately 265,000 women served in the US military during the Vietnam era, i.e., between 1964 and 1974. They were stationed in Guam, Japan, the Philippines, and Hawaii. There were two naval hospital ships carrying two registered nurses. The Vietnam Women's Memorial project reached many women and became known as the "Sister Search." It became very important for collecting data about all the women who served in Vietnam.

Few people realize how many nurses are needed to have a war. The Vietnam nurses were not safe behind enemy lines. Hospitals were bombed and rocketed, and nurses were killed. This was a war of firebase camps and guerilla warfare. This was no safe area for nurses. Many a night we stayed in bunkers, side by side with our brothers in arms. None of us walked away from this unscathed. Forty-eight percent of those women suffer from PTSD. The Boston Veterans Administration (VA) Center is the women's T okay leave as is center for PTSD. It is one of many in the country as of the 1980'S .My healing has been through many venues. I have been on TV in a production called *Focus on Health*. It consisted of a panel of nurses, one RN from the Korean War and three nurses from Vietnam. This was nationally televised. Once I told my story and my experiences as an OR nurse in a small town in Vietnam called Phu Bai, I began to reach out and explore my tour of duty more deeply.

Not all of the women continued in the field of nursing; many left nursing for good. They pursued other avenues of health care, e.g., administrative positions in the health field, social work, teaching nursing, or owning in spiritually focused shops.

Articles about me have been steady and frequent. I have appeared in the little capsule hospital newsletter, the *Boston Globe*, *Bay State Nurses* newsletter, *MetroWest*, and the *Lowell Sun*.

My inward healing has come from writing poems, painting about my experiences, and writing this book. I even helped produce a play. I have found that children and teens really learn from these types of expressions.

My poems have been sought out by journalists. Displays of my paintings about Vietnam were a part of a program titled *The Women of Vietnam Honor All Veterans* conference at the Museum of National Heritage, Lexington, MA, in 1995. I recited my poems as part of the display.

My experiences were also recognized on a talk-radio show. A physician from the Boston VA and I spoke about the PTSD that affected the women who served and also fielded questions from the audience.

Another history display was a mobile museum memorial that travelled across the country of articles, letters, bottles, tourniquets from the war, flowers, and anything dear to veterans' families. My contribution were OR tools and three very touching poems about an RN working in an operating room They are currently in a section of the mobile museum called "Memoirs of the Wall."

When I visited the Wall, I was moved to tears to see all the items left by the families and friends of the veterans and also so grateful to have a place to contribute my own memorial. I displayed my war-time paintings and recited poetry that I had written about Vietnam.

I hope you have been enriched by reading my story. I realize it's difficult to read but it is the only way for me to come home. This is the legacy of one little or nurse in Phu Bai, Vietnam.

Thank you for your interest in the female wartime experience in Vietnam. I never felt so needed, so brave, so loved by the GIs in Vietnam. They called me ma'am and carried me in their arms to the operating room when the red mud was one foot deep.

Thank you for your service of just your interest in combat nurses. No more Band-Aids on that open wound called PTSD. Let the light of reason shine on our glory, our sacrifice, our truth. I tried to bring the experience a voice and a true light. I am trying to bring my autobiography to open the door of Vietnam for all women who do not have a voice. My only hope is that this book has helped you in any way. Welcome my sisters, welcome home.

We need to tell our story lest someone else writes our memoirs for us. I need to thank you; it has been a difficult read. If you had to stop and put your head down, I am sorry. In all the darkness and horror I have shown light.

A special thanks to Kathleen Logan Harrod. She has been through it with me from the beginning. I have shed many a tear on her shoulder, she's brought me through the dark periods and throughout my healing process. I hope I have brought some light to the dark shadows.

Thank you to all the women who have served in the military. God bless you.

Bernadette Harrod RN, MSN

Appendix A: Letters of Support

Dear Bernadette:

Thank you so much for sharing your poems and art work at our Women Veterans Day Program on November 2, 1996. I can only imagine what courage it took—especially after I heard your poems and saw your paintings. It meant a great deal to me personally that you were able to attend. I know your efforts touched everyone there. I think you summed it all up by telling everyone there that you loved them. That really filled my heart.

I admire your work and you as a person.

Sincerely,
Pat Robinson, RN

******

Dear Bernadette:

Just a brief note to thank you for sharing your compelling story with our listeners. I only hope that continuing to share your story strengthens your conviction of how important your role really was. Along with many, I too had never listened or heard a women's viewpoint ... I'm glad I had an opportunity, it changed my perception completely.

I enclosed a tape for you. Thank you again for giving us a great show.

Sincerely,
Maryann Miller Brown OK

******

The Commonwealth of Massachusetts
Executive Office of Human Services
Office of Commissioner of Veterans' Services
Leverett Saltonstall Building, Government Center
100 Cambridge Street
Boston, MA 02202

March 22, 1985

Dear Ms. Harrod:

We wish to inform you that I have recommended your name for appointment to the Governor Advisory Committee on Women Veterans. Congratulations!

We are presently working to assemble the Committee as quickly as we can. When we have the nominees from all quarters, we will be contacting you with further information. Enclosed please find a copy of the legislation as it was signed.

We look forward to working with you on some very important questions including those addressing the apparent lack of interest in Women Veterans' issues. There is much work to be done. Again, congratulations!

    Sincerely,
    John Halachis
    Commissioner

******

Jim Kennedy
Framingham, MA

Dear Bernie,

Last Veteran's Day I went to the Wall for the first time. I went down with Richard Bouvier and a couple of other guys I don't think you know.

I was just a little choked up until I saw the Woman's Memorial. Blew me right away. I sprang a leak right then and there. I don't think I have ever been so moved. I wasn't the only one either. After a while I just stepped to the side and watched people as they came up to the memorial. There weren't many dry eyes. A lot of GIs are very very grateful for what you guys did—for the simple fact you were there.

When I was coming back on the train I was writing to a friend of mine about it. For some reason I thought of the Mormon belief that in the hour of your death your closest friends and loved ones who died before will come to escort your soul to heaven. For you combat nurses a lot of GIs would insist on being there. It would be a mob scene.

The picture I will include speaks for itself. The roses and flag were a perfect touch. I still tear up just looking at it.

Since it was my first time, there were a number of special moments. One particularly sticks in my mind. I was standing looking up at the wall. An attractive middle-aged woman was walking toward me from the side. I don't know what she saw in my face, but she stopped, looked up at me, and said simply, "Thank you." Then she walked on.

I wore your T-shirt down and will include a picture to prove it.

If you ever need a 50,000-mile check-up, give me a call. I am using a new technique called EMDR, which is showing some real promise [at] rooting out buried or difficult-to-get-out connections and traumas.

Tell Kathy hello for me.

Jim

Appendix B: The Statue

The dedication of the Vietnam Women's Memorial took place on November 11, 1993, in Washington, DC, near the Vietnam Veterans Memorial.

Glenna Goodacre's larger-than-life bronze sculpture consists of three fatigue-clad women; one woman is seated on a pile of sandbags cradling a wounded GI whose eyes are bandaged; one is kneeling, staring with "despair" into an empty helmet; and one is standing, her gaze turned anxiously toward the sky waiting for a medical evacuation helicopter.

The sculpture is a work of deception. It gives the false impression that American women were serving shoulder-to-shoulder with men in combat in Vietnam. They did not, and they certainly did not hang helplessly around sand-bagged bunkers, waiting for helicopters to haul our wounded men to some rear echelon for help.

They were the help. The nurses and doctors were the rear echelons. They were where the wounded were sent *to*, not *from*, for immediate care. Their medical units *were* the destination. There the GIs either recovered, were sent to rehab and then home, or were returned to their homeland in bags.

November 11, 1993, Veterans Day. To me, that date marks the dedication of the statue honoring the Vietnam nurses.

******

We didn't escape that war unscathed and unscarred. I'd like to have seen them fight that war without the nurses. We worked putting the soldiers back together. We got bombed. Our hospital took seven rockets. A nurse was killed there and half the hospital collapsed, Harrod said.

The Vietnam Women's Memorial Project got its start from two former Army nurses—Diane Carlson Evans, R.N., of River Falls, Wisc., and Donna-Marie Boulay, R.N., JD, who practices health law in Minneapolis. Both felt that this recognition would help teach the

American public about the role women had in the Vietnam War, as well as help those women in their healing process. In addition, they felt the memorial would serve to help locate and identify all the women who served in Vietnam. There is now no accurate record.

The committee was formed in 1984, and in three years has raised $300,000, has a pledge of $500,000 from a pharmaceutical firm. They hope to raise another $400,000 to reach their goal.

Noted Minnesota sculptor Roger M. Brodin was commissioned for the statue—a life-sized bronze sculpture of a woman wearing fatigues, combat boots, and a weary, yet compassionate expression. The statue is intended to stand as a symbol of woman as listener, nurturer, healer, spiritual leader and patriot. The committee now plans to ask Congress to override the Fine Arts Commission's disapproval so the statue can be dedicated on Veterans Day next year.

They urge supporters to write letters on personal stationery to President Ronald Reagan, their Congressional representatives and J. Carter Brown, 6th Ave. and Constitution, Washington, DC 20565. As director of the National Gallery of Art, Brown has jurisdiction over the monument.

******

"Memorial to Vietnam nurses dedicated today"
Middlesex News, Thursday, November 11, 1993

By Sharon Kahn

For two decades, Bernadette Harrod's memories of Vietnam festered. As a nurse at a hospital in Phu Bai near the city of Hue, she was a regular witness to the horrors of combat. Her job was to help the surgeons patch the broken bodies of the wounded soldiers who were brought in fresh from the battlefield. The goal was to keep the young men alive, even if only long enough to survive the trip to another hospital for advanced treatment.

Harrod's hospital was the front line of medical care. The soldiers never stayed more than 24 hours.

"We did life and limb surgery," said Harrod, 48, of Framingham. "We just cut off limbs and opened up bellies. It was the first stop for the wounded."

But in 1969, when Harrod came home after a year in Vietnam, nobody wanted to hear about the carnage, the young lives lost. And Harrod didn't want to tell.

"We were there alone. We felt alone and when we came home, we remembered alone," said Harrod, who teaches at St. Elizabeth's Hospital School of Nursing in Brighton.

It took years and the dedication of the Vietnam soldiers memorial for Harrod to find her voice.

"When the statue of three men went up it was missing one person and that was a female—a nurse," Harrod said.

She joined the Vietnam Women's Memorial Project, a grassroots effort to erect a statue honoring the 265,000 women who served during Vietnam.

Today the bronze statue will be dedicated at the Vietnam Veterans Memorial in Washington.

Harrod will be there, searching for the anonymous soldiers who she helped to heal.

"There has to be some closure. There has to be some healing and there has to be somewhere to go to celebrate the patriotism and the courage of the women who went," she said. "It will be a union of spirits and perhaps the miracle will happen for me and I will meet one of the nameless wounded soldiers I cared for."

Just look at the statue and you'll get an idea of what it was like. The sadness, the sense of urgency and the sense that we just won't be able to do enough.

******

Keynote Speaker
Brigadier General Wilma L. Vaught, USAF, ret.

Brigadier General Wilma L. Vaught, a Vietnam veteran and one of the most decorated military women, is President of the Board of Directors of the Women in Military Service for America Memorial Foundation, Inc., which seeks to raise funds for a memorial complex to be constructed at Arlington National Cemetery. The memorial will pay tribute to women veterans of all the service branches and eras.

A native of Illinois, General Vaught retired from the armed forces in 1985, having served as Commander of the United States Military Entrance Processing Command, North Chicago, Illinois, since 1982. During her military career, she held various posts both here and abroad. She served most recently as Chairperson of the NATO Women in the Allied Forces Committee from 1983 to 1985 and was the senior woman military representative to the Defense Advisory Committee on Women in the Services from 1982 to 1985.

General Vaught was the only woman to command a unit receiving the Joint Meritorious Unit Award, the highest peacetime unit award, and was the first woman to serve with a Strategic Air Command bombardment wing on operational deployment in 1966–67. Among her other military decorations and awards, General Vaught received the Air Force Distinguished Service Medal, the Air Force Legion of Merit, the Bronze Star Medal, the Meritorious Service Medal, the Joint Service Commendation Medal, the Air Force Commendation Medal with Oak Leaf Cluster, the Vietnam Service Medal with four stars, the Republic of Vietnam Gallantry Cross with palm and Republic of Vietnam Campaign Medal.

Since her retirement, she has lectured widely on leadership and management, as well as serving as a consultant to the Strategic Defense Initiative and to industry. She serves on the Board of Directors of the Air Force Retired Officers Community and on the Advisory Board of Women as Leaders in Washington, D.C.

General Vaught is also a member of the International Women's Forum, which presented her with the Woman Who Made A Difference Award in 1985. Her career is marked with many other distinctive achievements, including being the only woman to head the board of directors of a major credit union. General Vaught is listed in "Who's Who in America" and "Who's Who in American Women."

To Bernie

flags today in tribute wave
for those loyal ones who gave
of their youth their hopes their
might for a cause they knew
was right

morning bells sound their call
pause and say a prayer for all
who served valiantly that
men might be ever free

toll of bells, drum slow beat
silence falls in every street
in each heart swells the plea
keep us safe but keep us free

Written by the third-grade class at Potter Road School,
FRAMINGHAM MA. 1990

Dear Bernadette:

We are most grateful to you for submitting your poems to be considered for inclusion in our anthology: *Visions of War: Dreams of Peace*. After reviewing the material you submitted we would like to include the following works: "Even Now"

We came across your poem in the Joiner Center publication and would like very much to use it in our anthology. If you're not familiar with our project, we're both Vietnam Vets and have put together a collection of about 100 works by women who were in Vietnam during the war ...

We believe these are very powerful and poignant writings and we know that they will be important to the success of this work. We may have made some small editorial changes which we believe enhance the literary quality of the poem. However, we have included copies of the finished work for your review. If these changes are acceptable to you we would appreciate your permission to proceed with publication.

Enclosed please find the publishers "Permission to Reprint" form, which outlines the terms of our agreement. Please note in paragraph 3 that your $50 royalty fee will be donated, in your name, to the Vietnam Women's Memorial Project, as will all other royalties obtained from the sale of this book.

Copyright for your work will be obtained in your name by the publisher. In addition, upon publication we will send you a copy of the book.

We hope to include a short biographical sketch of each poet in the book, when you return the "Permission to Reprint" form, would you please enclose such a summary that includes your date and place of birth, assignment during the Vietnam War including rank, branch of service or occupation and agency affiliation if applicable. We will be glad to include any current information such as work activity, marital status, etc. and/or any other information you would like included. Please include the name and publisher of any other publications in which your work has appeared. If any of the specific poems we are using in this anthology have been published in another source, we do need the specifics so it can be credited in our book.

The scheduled publication date is Memorial Day, 1991. In order to meet the publishers deadline we need your response as quickly as possible.

Again we would like to thank you for being a part of what we believe will be a significant work and contribution to the literature of the Vietnam War.

******

December 6, 1995

Dear Bernadette,   (Re: Even now, after twenty years, I ...)

It is my pleasure to inform you that after reading and discussing your poem our Selection Committee has certified your poem as a semi-finalist in our 1995 North American Open Poetry Contest. Your poem will automatically be entered into the final competition held in Spring 1996. As a semi-finalist, you have an excellent chance of winning one of 70 cash or gift prizes—you may even win the $1,000.00 Grand Prize (a complete list of prizes can be found on one of the enclosures to this letter).

IMAGINE YOUR POEM ... PUBLISHED IN A BEAUTIFUL ANTHOLOGY!

And Bernadette, in view of your talent, we also wish to publish your poem in our forthcoming anthology ...

Beneath the Harvest Moon

Library of Congress ISBN 1-57553-063-5

Beneath the Harvest Moon, scheduled for publication in Summer of 1996, will be a classic, edition-quality hardbound volume, printed on fine milled paper to last for generations. It will make a handsome addition to any library, a treasured family keepsake, or a highly valued personal gift.

NO OBLIGATION WHATSOEVER

Before going any further, Bernadette, let me make one thing clear ... your poem was selected for publication, and as a contest semi-finalist, solely on the basis of merit. You are under no obligation whatsoever to submit any entry fee, any subsidy payment, or to make any purchase of any kind. Of course, many people do wish to own a copy of the publication in which their artistry appears. If this is the case, we welcome your order and guarantee your satisfaction. Please see the enclosed material for special discount information if you are interested in owning a copy of *Beneath the Harvest Moon.*

SO, WHAT HAPPENS NOW?

As I mentioned above, your poem has automatically been entered in the final competition—so you need take no action on the contest at this time. However, regarding the publication of your poem, you must complete the enclosed Author's Release stating that the poem you submitted is your original work of art, and that you give us permission to publish it ... I

Trend
The Way We Live

Supporting role
Framingham woman organizing group for women Vietnam vets

Appendix C: Forming Support Groups for Female Veterans

In the early stages of writing this book, I attempted to form a women's outreach group in MetroWest. As far as I knew, there were no groups at that time for female Vietnam veterans. They were having a hard time, and there was no place for them to go. Historically, women didn't go to veterans centers because they are male oriented. We needed to have women come forth and form such outreach groups. The discussions would center on the challenges women have in dealing with their Vietnam experience.

I flew home alone on a jumbo jet filled with soldiers who sat in silence and sadness. For me, coming home was a major blow. No one thanked us; there was no band, no bugle, no flag. There was nobody, absolutely nobody. I had expected to be honored. Instead, I was told to change from my uniform into civilian clothes in the airport restroom. It was a time when war protesters taunted those in uniform and made no exceptions for nurses. The country didn't go with us emotionally, nor did it embrace us on the way home. It was a tragedy.

I had expected some measure of understanding and respect from other professionals, but what I found were fellow nurses who didn't want to hear about Vietnam. Wearied and angered by insensitivity and ignorance, I took my experience in Phu Bai off my résumé after a while because I was tired of people asking me why I went. I also quickly realized that my clinical expertise wasn't well understood or valued. When I got back, I had to become certified to put in IVs, even though I could put in an IV in the dark under fire.

I felt the strong call to serve in Vietnam. I did it for God and country. I had to go. I went to Vietnam the way Florence Nightingale went to the Crimean War. I was always going to be a nurse. I was always going to go to a war. I couldn't not go.

Nurses experienced sexual harassment, another major cruelty of war. I knew of rape and harassment endured by nurses who never spoke about them until twenty years later. Others suffered from posttraumatic stress disorder and found no one to help.

My healing has been slow and painful, but the dedication of the Vietnam Women's Memorial was a major step. I'm very proud that I cared enough to put my life on the line and go over there. Writing has helped me put the pieces of my heart and soul back together. My poetry has been published in local newspapers, and one of my poems appears in the book *Visions of War, Dreams of Peace: Writings of Women in the Vietnam War*, edited by Linda Van Devanter and Joan Furey. I also paint in oils, and my works picture wartime themes. Recently, my artwork was displayed in the National Heritage Museum in Lexington.

Vietnam had a transformative effect on my life. Vietnam is not part of who I was, Vietnam is part of who I am, and it will never, never go away. What I did in a year, I haven't replicated in forty.

Bernie,

I hope you could be in D.C. for the dedication.
Thanks for serving from all us guys who loved & needed you.

J. Kennedy

Nursing her wounds with art.

Glossary

amp: amputation, to cut off a limb

ARVAN: South Vietnamese soldier.

breaking 100: Having only ninety-nine days left in country.

bunker: Protective steel housing surrounded by sand bags and ditches. You crawl to the bunker when rounds are coming in, and the siren blows.

bummer: Anything that went wrong; one of the top-ten sayings during the war.

crack a belly: To perform an abdominal operation, to open the belly surgically and look for bleeders or hemorrhage.

cherry: Someone who is new in country. One who has never been shot at or received any incoming rounds.

chopper bracelet: Whenever you became friendly with a chopper pilot, he would fashion a bracelet out of a chopper's stainless steel timing chain, size it to your wrist, cut it, and fasten it with a cotter pin. Voila! A war memento from a handsome chopper jockey.

Charlie, or VC; synonymous terms for the North Vietnamese Communist soldiers.

DEROS: Date Eligible for Return from Overseas. Everyone had a separate DEROS, thus the war was one of individuals coming in alone and leaving alone.

DMZ: The demilitarized zone between North and South Vietnam; located above Hue and Quang Tri.

dog tags: Two stamped identification tags on a metal chain worn around the neck. Tags had your name, unit, army number, and blood type. One tag was worn on your boot during Vietnam so that they could identify the body if the head were missing.

donuts or donut dollies: Female Red Cross workers. Educated, college women who volunteered to go to Vietnam for a year and help the soldiers through social interactions and group therapies.

dust off: A helicopter lifting off the ground, spewing dust everywhere.

EM: Enlisted man.

ETS: Estimated time of separation from service, the day you'd leave.

expectants: GIs who were fully expected to die were put aside in the triage area and left to die. Often expressed in numbers (6-12-2). The hardest duty was to be in charge of the expectant or "take out" area to offer comfort, a hand, or a word to a dying GI.

fatigues: Military combat wear. Solid green and blousy with combat boots. The marines had the camouflage. Your "cover" is your ball cap. For an in-look you could have the fatigues pegged at the PX.

firebase camp: The area of operations for the artillery and infantry in Vietnam. The war was conducted from various firebase camps rather than fought on a conventional battleground or front line.

flak jacket: A bulletproof vest that the nurses had to wear along with their helmets when they were traveling in country.

fly-bye: A military good-bye to someone who was leaving Vietnam. The helicopter pilot would buzz a low pass by the hospital helipad and emit color smoke bombs from his fuselage.

frag: A chip of metal or bullet lodged under the skin. It is a type of wound. To catch a frag is to be hit.

gooks: A derogatory term for the Vietnamese, which made them seem small and subhuman.

Graves Registration: The air-conditioned holding area for bodies and body parts. Probably the toughest assignment to pull in Nam.

Highway T: The main thoroughfare going through South Vietnam. It was a dirt road for convoys going south.

hooch: Place of domicile for the nurses. There were wooden structures for the EMs and nurses tents for the men.

hump day: Day 183 of your yearlong tour of duty.

I Corps: The area of northern South Vietnam where Phu Bai is located. Home for the First Air Cavalry Division and 101st Air Cavalry Division between Quang Tri and Duc Pho.

ICU: Intensive care unit.

IV: Intravenous; salt water or sugar water solutions that are pumped into the vein to prevent shock.

incoming: General term for being shot at.

in country: A general term for everyone in Vietnam.

in-country R&R: Places of relative quiet, where stand-downs occurred. Music, recreation, and beach facilities were available. Da Nang's China Beach was in-country R&R for us in I Corps.

klick: One kilometer; a metric measure of distance used by the military.

lift off: The general term for getting the wounded out of the bush. A Huey model chopper would medevac out the wounded directly to the surgical hospital.

Mama San: A Vietnamese woman who worked on the military post. Mama San washed your clothes and polished your and cleaned your quarters. Mama San was your personal maid for your stay.

Mars calls: Special telephone lines to the world that were available to patients. The telephone signals were transmitted via a naval ship in the South China Sea.

MPCs: Military script, "funny money." Military equivalent of a dollar so that hard US currency didn't infiltrate the Vietnamese economy.

Med Cap: A traveling health-care team of army nurses and doctors who visited villages when they were off duty, set up clinics, and treated the Vietnamese. It was sort of a traveling health screening team.

Medevac: Unit of helicopter pilots assigned to the surgical hospital. They would go out on a helicopter, pick up the wounded right where they were shot, and evacuate them to the surgical hospital.

midnight chow: The best meal of the day. A grill was set up, and you could have an army burger or breakfast cooked to order.

MUST: A medical unit, self-contained and transportable. Similar to the MASH units that were used during the Korean War.

NVA: North Vietnamese soldier.

OR: Operating room, usually four small collapsible structures joined together.

over the hump: All those days beyond the 183rd (see hump day).

PTSD: Posttraumatic stress syndrome, commonly called "shell shock," is a collection of symptoms suffered by those who have experienced the horrors of war and its consequences over prolonged time. The symptoms include insomnia, depression, dreams of flashbacks, alcoholism, and troubled relationships. The more subtle aspects of PTSD are a feeling of isolation, powerlessness, fear, and overwhelming sadness. The syndrome of PTSD worsens if there is an enforced silence around the trauma. The nurses who were in Vietnam were combat veterans with prolonged exposure to horrific injury, and then they were silent for decades about their traumatic experience.

perimeter: The guarded area of barbed-wire fencing where the US base stopped and Charlie country began.

Phu Bai: The city that farthest north in South Vietnam. Next to Hué on the cusp of the DMZ. Home of the Twenty-Second Surgical Hospital in I Corps.

push: When the casualties were numerous, we would operate nonstop until every case was done. Sometimes it would be thirty-six to forty-eight hours straight.

RA: Regular army career officers or "lifers."

RVN: Republic of Vietnam, namely South Vietnam.

round eye: Term for all American military and civilian women, including USO and Red Cross workers, in Vietnam.

short: Having just a few days left to serve in country.

short-timer: Any military person who was going home soon.

short-timers stick: A back swagger stick carried by short-timers. They would notch out the days with their knife. Some were bone color; some were black. Some were in the shape of a clenched hand denoting Black Power. Some were shaped in a fist with the middle finger up.

single-digit midget: The shortest of short with less than ten days. He or she was rendered sacrosanct and did not have to listen to any long stories as he or she was "too short."

Stars and Stripes: Military newspaper whose highlights included taking your malaria pills, watching out for VD, protecting yourself from jungle rot, and other tips on keeping healthy in a war zone.

brothers: Black soldiers.

Nam: "Hell"—all of the Vietnam experience.

world, the: The United States, back home.

Touchdown: The point when the medevac pilot landed on the helipad. The triage doctors and nurses met the chopper and transported the wounded soldiers to the triage area for assessment.

triage: A method of tagging or assigning priority to casualties.

watts line: Special telephone lines to the world. They were only open to the United States at certain times. We would wait in line for hours to talk. After every sentence you would have to say "over." Then the person on the other end could respond. It was awkward to send the messages: "I miss you, over." "I love you, over."

your cover: The unit's protective underground area where everyone went during attacks YES

two-digit midget: A short-timer who had less than one hundred days to serve out his YES assignment in Vietnam.

Twenty-Second Surg: A MUST in Phu Bai. Surgeries of life- and limb-saving nature were performed here. Once stable, the wounded were air-evacuated to Chu Lai in the midregion of Vietnam, or to one of the navy hospital boats, the *Repose* or the *Sanctuary*, afloat in international waters in the South China Sea.

Afterword

One of the women from the Vietnam Women's Memorial project called to find I was not at home. My husband, Dennis, answered, and they chatted for a moment. Somewhere she thought she had read he was a Viet vet and asked him. He said, yes, that he was. She said, "Good for you." After he hung up, he found that he was weeping. Later on, when he told me what had happened, his eyes began to fill with tears again. He said, "No one has ever said that to me." The healing process continues. It is not complete; it may never be. But it's not up to us to determine when it's over; the veteran is the only one who knows. We have acted as would-be healers, slapping a Band-Aid over a gaping wound and saying there, the pain is over. And the victims have been screaming, "No, I'm still bleeding. I'm still in pain." When are we going to hear them?

—Unknown

Printed in the United States
By Bookmasters